STEADFAST

Love

A STUDY OF PSALM 107

LAUREN CHANDLER

LifeWay Press®
Nashville, Tennessee

Published by LifeWay Press® • ©2017 Lauren Chandler

No part of this book may be reproduced or transmitted in any form or by any means, electronic or mechanical, including photocopying and recording, or by any information storage or retrieval system, except as may be expressly permitted in writing by the publisher. Requests for permission should be addressed in writing to LifeWay Press®; One LifeWay Plaza; Nashville, TN 37234-0152.

ISBN 978-1-4300-6052-9
Item 005787964
Dewey decimal classification: 223.2
Subject heading: LOVE \ GOD \ BIBLE. O.T. PSALMS 107—STUDY AND TEACHING

Unless otherwise noted, Scripture quotations are from the ESV® Bible (The Holy Bible, English Standard Version®, copyright © 2001 by Crossway, a publishing ministry of Good News Publishers. Used by permission. All rights reserved. Scripture passages marked MSG taken from THE MESSAGE, Eugene Peterson, Copyright © 1993, 1994, 1995, 1996, 2000, 2001, 2002, Used by Permission of NavPress. All Rights reserved. www.navpress. com Represented by Tyndale House Publishers, Inc. (1.800.366.7788). Scripture quotations marked CSB have been taken from the Christian Standard Bible®, Copyright ©2017 by Holman Bible Publishers. Used by permission. Christian Standard Bible® and CSB® are federally registered trademarks of Holman Bible Publishers. Scripture quotations marked (NIV) are taken from The Holy Bible, New International Version®, NIV® Copyright © 1973, 1978, 1984, 2011 by Biblica, Inc.™ Used by permission of Zondervan. All rights reserved worldwide. www.zondervan.com. The "NIV" and "New International Version" are trademarks registered in the United States Patent and Trademark Office by Biblica, Inc.™

To order additional copies of this resource, write LifeWay Church Resources Customer Service; One LifeWay Plaza; Nashville, TN 37234-0113; FAX order to 615.251.5933; call toll-free 800.458.2772; email orderentry@lifeway.com; order online at LifeWay.com; or visit the LifeWay Christian Store serving you.

Printed in the United States of America.
Adult Ministry Publishing, LifeWay Church Resources,
One LifeWay Plaza, Nashville, TN 37234-0152

TABLE OF CONTENTS

ABOUT THE AUTHOR

Lauren Chandler is a wife and mother of three. Her husband, Matt Chandler, serves as the lead teaching pastor at The Village Church in Dallas, Texas. Lauren is passionate about writing, music, and leading worship, not only at The Village Church, but also for groups across the country. The Lord has taken Matt and Lauren on a challenging journey, beginning with the November 2009 discovery of a malignant brain tumor in Matt. The Lord has been infinitely merciful to provide peace and comfort in uncertainty and joy in times of victory and healing. Lauren and her family have been given a deeper trust in clinging to the Lord and His cross during this appointed season of valleys and storms.

INTRODUCTION

I grew up a church girl. From the Cradle Roll to Graduation Sunday, I rarely missed a Sunday morning sitting on a wooden pew beside my father, mother, and little brother. Squirming in a starched dress and suffocating stockings, I would catch my mother's correcting glare and surrender to an hour of big words on bulletins. Now, this is all from the perspective of an elementary student who grasped more of the gospel through songs and Bible stories in Sunday School than through Mrs. Williford's solos and Dr. Hall's sermons. The gospel was there; my little heart and mind just didn't have the capacity to catch it—yet. It was (and is) an important practice to sit as a family and hear the Word sung and preached.

But back to those big words on bulletins. If you didn't grow up a church kid or your church was of a different denomination, you may have tripped over the word *bulletin*. What in the world is that? The bulletin was a piece of paper on which the order of worship was printed for all to follow along. Think of it as a less lustrous Playbill; but instead of "Act One" there were words like *invocation, invitation,* and *benediction.* The invitation is as it sounds: a chance for those who heard the sermon to respond, either by putting their faith in Christ, receiving prayer, or deciding to join the church. The benediction came at the end of the service. It was a time to receive and bestow a blessing—a time to remind each other that, for the believer, "the grace of the Lord Jesus Christ and the love of God and the fellowship of the Holy Spirit [would] be with [each of us]" (2 Cor. 13:14). I saved the term invocation for last because I want this concept to stick with you for the rest of the week. To *invoke* means "to call for with earnest desire."[1] This is why the invocation may also be termed the "call to worship."

At the beginning of a praise and worship service, the invocation may be interpreted two different (although often happening simultaneously) ways. One may view the call to worship as a corporate prayer to the Lord to make His presence manifest among them. We know God is omnipresent. King David penned a psalm describing God's inescapable presence. He could go down to the depths and God would be there. He could climb upon the heights and still, God would be there (Ps. 139). But there were also times when David, although he knew God's presence remained, had a hard time perceiving Him (Ps. 71:12). As Christians, we are sealed with the Holy Spirit—He takes residence within us—so He certainly isn't far. But aren't there times when you want to experience His manifest presence? When you want to "feel"

His nearness? When a word preached or spoken or sung hits square in that tender spot? That's the heart behind this interpretation of invocation. We are calling upon the Lord to come closer—close enough to feel His breath, smell His scent, and hear His heartbeat.

While it is certainly good—it's even encouraged in Scripture—to ask God to draw nearer to us as we draw near to Him (Jas. 4:8), the call to worship can also be an opportunity for the worship leader or pastor to implore the congregation to "come closer."

Let's face it. Who among us hasn't stumbled into a worship service with the cares of the week heavy on our shoulders, or with sleepy eyes and foggy brains, or maybe simply out of duty because we sure haven't felt Him for quite a while? Most often we are the ones who need to be invoked—drawn out, called for with earnest desire.

I don't know how you're coming into this Bible study. I wish I could know what shape your spiritual life is in. I wish I could sit across from you at my favorite coffee shop and hear you pour out your heart. I know as many of you as there are, there are just as many different shapes and stories. Some of you are eager to jump right in—your spiritual life is vibrant and you are humming along smoothly on all cylinders. Some of you are cautiously stepping forward—this whole God thing is new to you, or it's been a long time since you've tried a Bible study. You have been hurt or simply dropped off the attendance roll and never had the courage to peek back in. Others of you are limping or crawling into this. You are barely getting by. Every morning is a painful reality that you are still here and so is the loss.

Friend, there is good news. The God of every season, the God over every storm, the God who loves you no matter the state of your spiritual health is here—ready and waiting for you. Yes, we can call out to God to make His presence manifest among us, but we can also be assured that He is right here waiting for us.

Psalm 107 is a call to worship—a call to the people of God to remember all the ways He has rescued and will continue to rescue. The psalmist is imploring the people to speak out loud of His faithfulness and thank Him for it. He invites us to invite each other to tell it. Because some of us need to hear a certain word right now, and all of us need to be reminded that God is here.

So I am inviting you to remember with me. The things we "remember" together may not be shared memories from our own stories but rather remembering how God has been faithful in history—in His story, for our stories are woven into His. I am asking God to make His presence manifest among us over the next seven weeks. But more importantly, I am reminding you (and myself) that He is already there, ready and waiting.

PSALM 107

1 Oh give thanks to the LORD, for he is good, for his steadfast love endures forever!

2 Let the redeemed of the LORD say so, whom he has redeemed from trouble

3 and gathered in from the lands, from the east and from the west, from the north and from the south.

4 Some wandered in desert wastes, finding no way to a city to dwell in;

5 hungry and thirsty, their soul fainted within them.

6 Then they cried to the LORD in their trouble, and he delivered them from their distress.

7 He led them by a straight way till they reached a city to dwell in.

8 Let them thank the LORD for his steadfast love, for his wondrous works to the children of man!

9 For he satisfies the longing soul, and the hungry soul he fills with good things.

10 Some sat in darkness and in the shadow of death, prisoners in affliction and in irons,

11 for they had rebelled against the words of God, and spurned the counsel of the Most High.

12 So he bowed their hearts down with hard labor; they fell down, with none to help.

13 Then they cried to the LORD in their trouble, and he delivered them from their distress.

14 He brought them out of darkness and the shadow of death, and burst their bonds apart.

15 Let them thank the LORD for his steadfast love, for his wondrous works to the children of man!

16 For he shatters the doors of bronze and cuts in two the bars of iron.

17 Some were fools through their sinful ways, and because of their iniquities suffered affliction;

18 they loathed any kind of food, and they drew near to the gates of death.

19 Then they cried to the LORD in their trouble, and he delivered them from their distress.

20 He sent out his word and healed them, and delivered them from their destruction.

21 Let them thank the LORD for his steadfast love, for his wondrous works to the children of man!

22 And let them offer sacrifices of thanksgiving, and tell of his deeds in songs of joy!

23 Some went down to the sea in ships, doing business on the great waters;

24 they saw the deeds of the Lord, his wondrous works in the deep.

25 For he commanded and raised the stormy wind, which lifted up the waves of the sea.

26 They mounted up to heaven; they went down to the depths; their courage melted away in their evil plight;

27 they reeled and staggered like drunken men and were at their wits' end.

28 Then they cried to the Lord in their trouble, and he delivered them from their distress.

29 He made the storm be still, and the waves of the sea were hushed.

30 Then they were glad that the waters were quiet, and he brought them to their desired haven.

31 Let them thank the Lord for his steadfast love, for his wondrous works to the children of man!

32 Let them extol him in the congregation of the people, and praise him in the assembly of the elders.

33 He turns rivers into a desert, springs of water into thirsty ground,

34 a fruitful land into a salty waste, because of the evil of its inhabitants.

35 He turns a desert into pools of water, a parched land into springs of water.

36 And there he lets the hungry dwell, and they establish a city to live in;

37 they sow fields and plant vineyards and get a fruitful yield.

38 By his blessing they multiply greatly, and he does not let their livestock diminish.

39 When they are diminished and brought low through oppression, evil, and sorrow,

40 he pours contempt on princes and makes them wander in trackless wastes;

41 but he raises up the needy out of affliction and makes their families like flocks.

42 The upright see it and are glad, and all wickedness shuts its mouth.

43 Whoever is wise, let him attend to these things; let them consider the steadfast love of the Lord.

A CALL TO WORSHIP

Oh give thanks to the LORD, for he is good,
    for his steadfast love endures forever!
Let the redeemed of the LORD say so,
    whom he has redeemed from trouble
and gathered in from the lands,
    from the east and from the west,
    from the north and from the south.

PSALM 107:1-3

Welcome to the *Steadfast Love* Bible study! Each week, I've provided some discussion questions here to get the conversation started. Feel free to discuss what you learned throughout the week of study, ask any questions you may have, and share what God is teaching you.

DISCUSSION QUESTIONS:

Read Psalm 107 aloud.

Which section of the psalm stands out to you? Explain.

What do you think of when you hear the term "Call to Worship"?

What drew you to this study? What do you hope to learn?

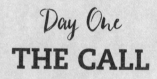

Day One
THE CALL

READ PSALM 107. Yes, all of it. If possible, out loud. This will take you two to three minutes at the most. (I timed it.)

With which section of the psalm can you most readily identify?

Which section is puzzling?

Think back to the video and introduction. Psalm 107 is described as a
_____ to _____.

We talked about "big words on bulletins." Which one means "to call with earnest desire"? (circle one)
☐ Invitation
☐ Invocation
☐ Benediction

We can invoke the Lord to "come closer," but we can also keep in mind that He is already there waiting for us to draw near to Him that He may draw near to us (Jas. 4:8). How have you come into the Bible study? Are you sprinting, jogging, dragging your feet, or crawling? Why? Be specific. Be honest. God already knows. Sometimes we need to put pen to paper to let ourselves know!

Let me level the playing field. The reality is that we are all on the same footing. We are all in need of Jesus. Every last one of us (yours truly included, if not more so than most).

> Turn to Galatians 2:16 and complete the following:
> "... yet we know that a person is not _____ by _____ of the law but through _____ in _____ _____ ..."

> Define justify (grab a dictionary or use a dictionary app on your device). Choose the definition that most likely fits in this context.

> Try writing the verse in your own words:

I'll move my cover sheet over to let you peek at my answer: *No one is made right by what they do but by believing that what Jesus has done for them is enough. We can't earn it, we can only receive it.*

What did Jesus do for us? I've heard it summarized like this, "Jesus lived the life I couldn't live and died the death I should have died."[1]

> Let's mine the Scriptures for this truth (write out the verses word-for-word or in your own words):

> Galatians 3:10

> Galatians 3:13

> Ephesians 2:8-9

Christ lived a sinless life that is impossible for me to live. He didn't keep it to Himself though. His obedience made me (and anyone who trusts in Him) righteous. And not only that, He willingly took my place in the shameful death on a cross that I deserved to die.

No matter how you've come to this study, we're all in the same boat. The only difference is that some of us may know the truth of our need for gospel grace more than others. But you can't tell from the outside. There may be those who are sprinting to the finish with medals dangling around their necks. This is just another "check" to put by a long list of works that we use to try to earn favor with God. Listen, I have been there. Don't fool yourself—you will grow tired. Your works are not enough. Others of you may be scraping along, barely clawing forward but fully convinced that every bit of progress is by the grace of God. You are leaning heavily on Christ for every breath. I have been there too. Don't despise these days; God is doing a deep work in you. Most of you are probably somewhere in between. Welcome.

> *Write a prayer of confession, surrender, gratitude, or whatever cry is in your heart.*

We start on the same footing responding to the same call. God is here, ready and waiting for us. Will you come closer?

Day Two
TO WORSHIP

Break out your dictionaries again! Write down the first three or four definitions for worship *below.*

I appreciate that *dictionary.com* frames worship as mostly a religious activity (because it is), but it doesn't exclusively occur inside the walls of a church, synagogue, or mosque.[2] Worship is the air we breathe. In other words, if we're breathing, we're worshiping. Now, the question is *what* or *whom* are we worshiping?

To worship means to have our mind's attention and heart's affection focused supremely on an object or person.[3] This doesn't have to be a deity. It can be absolutely anything.

Ask yourself the following questions to discern the object of your worship (answer with gut-level responses, not with what "should" be your answer):

What occupies your mind the most?

What do you love?

What can absolutely ruin your day?

What can absolutely make your day?

All of us have something that occupies our minds, has our love, can ruin our day, or make our day. It's part of being human. It's part of being created in the *Imago Dei,* the image of God.

Turn to Genesis 1:26-27 and write out the verses in the space below.

Genesis 1:1-25 recounts the story of creation—light, dark, heavens, earth, sky, waters, vegetation, fish, birds, creeping things, beasts of the earth, and livestock. (I'm convinced horses were one of the last to be created because they're my favorite. Jesus returns riding on a white one; I'm just saying.) Finally, He makes man (male and female). Mankind is distinguished from the rest of God's creatures in how we resemble God, represent Him in the world, and relate to Him and one another.

How do we resemble God? How do we not?

What does a representative do? How might we represent God simply by being human (not necessarily Christians)?

How were we created to relate with God and each other? (Hint: read Gen. 2:15-25.)

How is mankind doing at all of this? How are you? Not awesome, right? Even if you love God and seek to worship Him, it's a struggle to resemble, represent, and relate with Him in a way that honors Him, isn't it?

There's good reason for this. It's called the fall and it happened in Genesis 3. The serpent deceived Eve while Adam stood beside her doing nothing to prevent the worst catastrophe in the history of man. We will get into the ins and outs of this exchange later in the study, but for now, let's focus on its consequences. The bottom line is that the *Imago Dei* was marred and all creation suffered. Adam and Eve's choice to believe the serpent over God resulted in a fracture that makes resembling, representing, and relating with God in the way He intentioned impossible on our own.

Instead of simply resembling Him, we want to *be* Him. Instead of being His representatives on the earth, we abuse and exploit creation for our consumption. Instead of relating with God and each other from a place of being freely loved and freely loving, shame and selfishness infiltrate every relationship.

Essentially, we replace the Creator with the created. Our worship is broken but it's not extinct. We are still worshiping something.

Whatever your heart clings to and confides in, that is really your God, your functional savior.[4]

MARTIN LUTHER

When I first read "confides in," I immediately thought of a line in *The Golden Girls'* theme song. You know, the lyric that says, "Your heart is true, you're a pal and a confidant." It took me years to finally understand the last word. A confidant? What is that? Then, as I grew to have sensitive information about myself and others, I understood what it meant to confide—to trust someone with the deep and the dark. Although "confides" certainly means that here, it can also mean putting our trust in someone or something—much like how I "confided" in the chair I'm currently sitting on to be strong enough to hold me.

What are some things (or people) in which you "confide" or find stability?

After the fall, not only are we now more prone to worship and confide in something other than God, creation itself groans. Pain, suffering, and death plague us. We are desperate to find something that can sustain us, especially on darker days. Throughout the rest of this study, I will be using the image of the anchor to represent the object of our worship—that which we cling to and confide in. The anchor symbolizes hope and stability in the uncertain current of a post-Genesis 3 world.

In our broken worship, we tie our hope to false anchors—people or things that don't have the strength to save us. My prayer for you in this study is that you will let God use the seasons of pain, struggle, and uncertainty to expose the false anchors. And in exposing the false, I pray you are able to see, cling to, and confide in the true Anchor—the God of steadfast love.

Day Three
THE LORD

Write your name here:

Do you know the meaning of your name? If so, what is it? If not, take a few minutes to do a little research online (if you're "unplugged," come back to this exercise and complete it later).

Have you ever gone by another name? This is a mental exercise (you're welcome). Do some names recall good memories and emotions, and others not so good?

Growing up, my parents called me "Boo-Boo" or "Boo" for short. I'm not exactly sure where the name originated but it's always been a term of endearment. In fact, Matt and I call our girls "Boo" too. I can recall other names given to me, one in particular that I acquired during junior high. As with many junior high memories, I'm sure you can imagine that it stirs up awkward, anxious, and self-conscious feelings. I still have a complex over the body part this name mocked! To be fair, I cringe over the teasing I dispensed at that time in my life. I was by no means only a victim!

Names are powerful, aren't they? They may evoke various feelings and moments that have been seared in our minds—for better or worse. They help *define* and *distinguish* the named. So if our "names" have less than pleasing meanings or connotations, they can negatively mark our perceptions of ourselves and how we feel we are perceived by others. Likewise, if our names mean something profound or pleasant, we tend to flourish under their influence.

Names are a big deal to God. In various places throughout Scripture, He took the initiative to change a person's name to signify a new thing He was doing in and through that person.

Fill out the following table using the Scriptures listed in each row as a reference:

SCRIPTURE	ORIGINAL NAME	MEANING	NEW NAME	MEANING
Genesis 17:5		Exalted father		Father of a multitude
Genesis 17:15		Princess		Princess
Genesis 25:26; 32:28		Takes by the heel; he cheats; supplanter[5]		He strives with God, or God strives
John 1:40-42		He (God) has heard[6]		Rock
Acts 13:9		Asked/ prayed for[7]		Little or small[8]

Saul is an outlier among the others. He did not have a "you shall no longer be called" moment with God. From what we know in Scripture, it appears he chose to go by his Roman name, Paul.

> *Knowing that the name "Saul" is of Hebrew origin and "Paul," Roman, why do you think he chose to go by his Roman name? (See Acts 13:44-49.)*

Paul recognized the call of God on his life to proclaim the gospel to the Gentiles (non-Jews). Paul's name change signified his acceptance and made him more accessible to those to whom he'd been called.[9] That Paul means "little or small" endears him that much more to me. It echoes what he wrote to the Christians in Corinth:

- -

> *But he said to me, "My grace is sufficient for you, for my power is made perfect in weakness." Therefore I will boast all the more gladly of my weaknesses, so that the power of Christ may rest upon me.*

2 CORINTHIANS 12:9

- -

God has given Himself names that define an aspect of His character that makes Him relatable to us.

NAMES OF GOD

Look up the Scriptures listed below and complete the table. (Aren't these fun?)

SCRIPTURE	NAME OF GOD	HEBREW NAME
Genesis 14:18		El Elyon[10]
Genesis 17:1-2		El Shaddai[11]
Exodus 3:14; 6:2		Yahweh[12]

We could fill pages with names for God mentioned in the Bible but I want to home in on the last one in the table—Yahweh. Most often, it is translated as *the LORD* in English.

Read Exodus 6:2-8. To whom did God reveal His name the LORD (Yahweh)?

Who knew Him by another name? Which name?

What were God's people experiencing when He revealed His name Yahweh (see v. 5)?

Circle every time you see the word "I." Underline the action verbs (a verb that expresses mental or physical action).

- -

Say therefore to the people of Israel, "I am the LORD, and I will bring you out from under the burdens of the Egyptians, and I will deliver you from slavery to them, and I will redeem you with an outstretched arm and with great acts of judgment. I will take you to be my people, and I will be your God, and you shall know that I am the LORD your God, who has brought you out from under the burdens of the Egyptians. I will bring you into the land that I swore to give to Abraham, to Isaac, and to Jacob. I will give it to you for a possession. I am the LORD."

EXODUS 6:6-8

- -

Who is doing most of the acting in the passage above?

Yahweh, the LORD, is God's covenant-making and covenant-keeping name. He is reminding His people that He has not forgotten about them. He has heard their groaning. He knows their oppression. And He is about to do something about it. In Psalm 107, Yahweh is the name the psalmist chooses to use. I like to think that he is reminding God's people that the LORD—Yahweh—will deliver, free, and redeem those who cry out to Him.

The very next verse after God tells Moses all He will do for His people says, "Moses spoke thus to the people of Israel, but they did not listen to Moses, because of their broken spirit and harsh slavery" (Ex. 6:9).

Lord, let it not be so of us. May we not miss hearing Your promise to deliver because our ears are more attune to our brokenness and pain. May we cry out to the LORD—the One who is who He says He is and will do what He says He will do.

Where are you? Can you hear His promise to deliver over your brokenness and pain? Or is His voice drowned out? Write a prayer of confession. Confess where you are and where you want to be.

Day Four
COVENANT

Yesterday, we talked about God revealing the fullness of His name, Yahweh, the LORD, to the Israelites just before He delivered them from Egypt. We learned this is His "covenant-making and covenant-keeping" name. *Covenant* is a word we rarely use in modern times but the Bible is thick with it. So let's break out our dictionaries again. (We went a whole day without it!)

Define covenant:

The *Holman Illustrated Bible Dictionary* tells us that a *covenant* is an:

Oath-bound promise whereby one party solemnly pledges to bless or serve another party in some specified way. Sometimes the keeping of the promise depends upon the meeting of certain conditions by the party to whom the promise is made. On other occasions the promise is made unilaterally and unconditionally. The covenant concept is a central, unifying theme of Scripture, establishing and defining God's relationship to man in all ages.[13]

The Bible dictionary goes on to explain that the Hebrew word translated as *covenant* in the Old Testament is closely linked to the Hebrew word for *bind*. So, a covenant is an arrangement in which two parties are bound together.[14] It is an important theme of Scripture.

Let's look at several covenants throughout Scripture. I've filled in all the blanks for the first one, but I'll let you fill in some of the blanks for the others.

EDENIC COVENANT: GENESIS 2:15-17

Party 1: *God*
Party 2: *Adam*
Initiator: *God*
Promise: *Eat of any tree in the garden except for the tree of the knowledge of good and evil and thus have everlasting life.*
Condition: *Don't eat of the tree of the knowledge of good and evil or you'll die.*
Is there a method of restoration? *No*

COVENANT OF GRACE: GENESIS 3:14-15 (FOCUSING ON V. 15)

Party 1:
Party 2: *Mankind*
Initiator:
Promise: *Eve's offspring would crush the head of the serpent's offspring.*
Condition: *None*
Who might Eve's offspring be (Col. 2:13-15)?

NOAHIC COVENANT: GENESIS 9:8-17

Party 1:
Party 2: *Noah, his offspring, and every living creature with him*
Initiator:
Promise:

Condition: *None*
Sign of the covenant:

ABRAHAMIC COVENANT: GENESIS 12:1-3

Party 1:
Party 2:
Initiator:
Promise:

Condition: *Go*

In Genesis 15, God ratified His covenant with Abraham. He employed a practice common in Abraham's day. He instructed Abraham to cut several animals in two and lay them directly apart from each other on the ground, creating a path between the pieces. The custom required the parties to walk through the severed animals signifying, "may this be done to me if I do not keep the covenant."[15] Instead of both parties walking through the pieces, only God (symbolized by a smoking fire pot and torch) passed through.[16]

What is Abraham doing in 15:12?

Abraham was in the most vulnerable, helpless state when God made His covenant with him. And God didn't make him sleepwalk through the animal carcasses. Instead, He alone tread the path declaring, "may this be done to me, if this covenant is not kept."

How might this relate to Him being called "Yahweh"?

MOSAIC COVENANT: EXODUS 19:5-6

Party 1: *God*
Party 2: *Moses and the Israelites*
Initiator:
Promise:

Condition:

Again, as with Abraham, the Lord incorporated a custom familiar to Moses and His people. Suzerain treaties were pledges by a suzerain (king or overlord) "to provide benevolent rule and protection to conquered peoples in exchange for their loyalty."[17] The difference was that God did not "conquer" these people; He graciously extended His steadfast love to them. His commandments were not meant to be a burden but a picture of what He meant life to look like for human flourishing.

DAVIDIC COVENANT: 2 SAMUEL 7:7-16

Party 1:
Party 2:
Initiator:
Promise: *Your throne shall be established forever.*
Condition:

Read Romans 1:1-4. Who is a King descended from David?

NEW COVENANT: JEREMIAH 31:31-34

Party 1:
Party 2:
Initiator:
Promise: *Put my law within them; write it on their hearts; I will be their God and they will be my people; they will know me; I will forgive their iniquity and remember their sin no more*
Condition:

Complete the following from 2 Corinthians 1:20:

For _____ the _____ of God find their _____ in _____.

Christ fulfilled every covenant for us. He perfectly obeyed all of the Father's commands. He defeated death. He is the promised seed who would crush the serpent's head. He is the promised Son who would be a blessing to all nations. He kept the law of Moses and became an empathetic High Priest. He is the King who descended from David and sits enthroned forever. He instituted the new covenant.

I realize this day's study may have made some giggle with glee and others struggle to trudge through biblical history. I get it. My aim for homework today is to help you see God as the covenant-initiating and covenant-maintaining God. I want you to see that what He said He would do, He has done. There's still more to come. All is not as it will be. We still struggle against sin. Death has yet to finally die. Pain remains a part of life. But we can trace the goodness of God in keeping His promises throughout history so that we can trust He will keep His promise to be "with [us] always, to the end of the age" (Matt. 28:20) and that Christ has not left us. He will return (Acts 1:11).

Day Five

REDEEMED FROM THE HAND OF THE ENEMY

On Day Two, we discussed our brokenness as human beings—our broken worship, our innate tendency to cling to and confide in false anchors. We can be our own worst enemy. We can lie to ourselves. We can heap shame upon ourselves. Without Jesus, we are (to quote the artist Pink) a hazard to ourselves. But we're not our only enemy.

Give thanks to the LORD, for he is good;
his faithful love endures forever.
Let the redeemed of the LORD proclaim
that he has **redeemed them from the power of the foe**
and has gathered them from the lands—
from the east and the west,
from the north and the south.

PSALM 107:1-3, CSB **(emphasis mine)**

We have a somewhat daunting task today. We are going to (try to) tackle the (very real) topic of Satan—the enemy, or foe, of our souls. Some of us are strangely fascinated with the supernatural while others wouldn't touch it with a ten-foot pole. There can be error in both. We can make too much of Satan and demons—giving them more credit than they're due; or we can deny their existence altogether—choosing to ignore a large chunk of Scripture. My aim is to offer you a balanced, biblical view of "the power of the foe."

THE ENEMY OUTSIDE

Read Genesis 3:1-13. Focusing on verse 1, what do we know about the serpent from this verse?

Let's take a look at the dialogue between the serpent and Eve:

"Did God actually say, 'You shall not eat of any tree in the garden'?"

GENESIS 3:1

What did God actually say?

And the Lord God commanded the man, saying, "You may surely eat of every tree of the garden, but of the tree of the knowledge of good and evil you shall not eat, for in the day that you eat of it you shall surely die."

GENESIS 2:16-17

What did Eve say God said? Was she correct? Why, or why not?

What was the consequence for eating from the tree (Gen. 2:17)?

How did the serpent respond? (complete the following)

But the serpent said to the woman, "You will not surely die. For God knows that when you eat of it your eyes will be opened, and _____ will be _____ _____, knowing good and evil." Genesis 3:4-5

How do you think Eve felt about God after hearing this? How would you have felt?

Was the serpent right? Explain.

How did Adam and Eve respond to having their eyes opened?

Did the serpent make Adam and Eve take the fruit?

List the three things Eve noticed about the fruit (v. 6):
1.

2.

3.

According to James 1:14, how is each person tempted?

What's interesting is that Eve's desires alone weren't evil. How she looked to fulfill those desires was evil. God gave Adam and Eve everything they needed and more in the garden.

Read Genesis 2:9 and complete the following:

And out of the ground the L<small>ORD</small> God made to spring up every tree that is _____ to the _____ and _____ _____ _____. The tree of life was in the midst of the garden, and the tree of the knowledge of good and evil.

What about obtaining wisdom, you ask? How did God provide that in the garden? God is wisdom. What He told them about the tree of the knowledge of good and evil was wisdom—don't eat it or you will die. Would it have been wise for them to have obeyed and avoided it? Yes! We wouldn't be in this whole mess if they had!

But what about death? Did God get His bluff in?

James 1:15 goes on to say, "Then desire when it has conceived gives birth to sin, and sin when it is fully grown brings forth death." Eve looked for her desire to be fulfilled in the wrong thing, which birthed disobedience (taking the fruit and eating it). For a moment it seemed the serpent was right; they didn't die immediately. But the life they knew came to an immediate end. They no longer enjoyed fellowship with God and with each other. For the first time ever, they knew shame and hid from God; they lied and played the blame game. The gates to Eden were closed to them, the tree of life guarded by a flaming sword. The countdown to physical death started with the first bite of the forbidden fruit.

The serpent used his wiles to accomplish his will for Adam and Eve. Believe me, he has a will for your life too. He is a thief who comes "only to steal and kill and destroy" (John 10:10). He is our adversary who "prowls around like a roaring lion, seeking someone to devour" (1 Pet. 5:8). But, praise God, "we are not ignorant of his designs" (2 Cor. 2:11).

Satan doesn't have a new bag of tricks. He uses the same old designs or schemes. Let's take a peek into his bag:

1. He pretends to be your friend. ("He said to the woman …")

2. He prompts you to question what God says and who He is. ("Did God actually say …")

3. He appeals to our desires. ("The woman saw that the tree was good for food …")

4. He provokes you to take matters into your own hands. ("She took of its fruit and ate …")

5. His path leads to death. ("Therefore the LORD God sent him out …")

Is there an area of your life where you feel you're somewhere stuck in his bag of tricks? Put a star by any (or all) of the above schemes/designs that resonate with you. Feel free to expound.

What lies about God have you been led to believe?

THAT ANCIENT SERPENT, THE ACCUSER, AND JOB

You may be asking, what does the serpent have to do with Satan? He's not called Satan here. Revelation 20:2 makes the connection: "He seized the dragon, that ancient serpent, who is the devil and Satan, and bound him for a thousand years." Pretty direct statement.

He is the deceiver, accuser, tempter, and enemy of our souls. Unlike ninety-nine percent of Hollywood's interpretations of him, he is not on equal footing with God. He is created. God is uncreated—no one made Him. Now, that can open up a whole litany of questions. Why would God make Satan? Why would He allow evil? There's always an element of mystery with the Lord. As much as He has revealed about Himself in Scripture, our thoughts are not His thoughts, and our ways are not His ways (Isa. 55:8). What we can do is look at another interaction between God, Satan, and a human.

Job was an outstanding man. Job 1:1 says, "that man was blameless and upright, one who feared God and turned away from evil." He fathered seven sons and three daughters. His estate included seven thousand sheep, three thousand camels, five hundred yoke of oxen, five hundred female donkeys, and many servants. He was "the greatest of all the people of the east" (Job 1:3). Needless to say, he was a man surely blessed.

Read Job 1:6-22. Who mentioned Job first?

How does Satan respond to God's statement about Job? What is his accusation against Job?

How does God respond?

Satan had to ask permission to sift Job. That's part terrifying and part comforting. Terrifying that the Lord would allow something hard into my life; yet comforting to know Satan isn't running unchecked. John Piper aptly calls him "a lion on a leash."[18] The Lord tells Satan how far he can go and he can go no further.

Fast-forward to the end of the Book of Job.

Read Job 42:10-17. How does it end for Job?

Satan didn't know what the end would hold, but God did. Job didn't know how it would all turn out, but God did. There's a song we sing at our church with a bridge that reminds us, "Even what the enemy means for evil, You turn it for our good."[19]

We may not be at the place where we can see "the good." We might be smack-dab in the middle of the hard. But we can remember that Satan is merely a pawn in God's hand. Not only that, Satan has been checkmated. He may still have moves to make on the board, but Colossians 2:15 tells us that he has been ultimately defeated by Christ. For the Christian, we can trust that "all things work together for good" (Rom. 8:28).

Whew, friend. This was a doozy of a day of homework. So much here and yet so much more we could cover. I want to leave you with this: There is a very real enemy of your soul who wants to do everything he can to trick you into trusting false anchors and make you question the strength of the True Anchor. Do not be dismayed, though—he has been defeated, and no matter the schemes he designs for you, the Lord can turn it for your good.

God is the great Redeemer.

Week Two

THE DESERT

Some wandered in desert wastes,
    finding no way to a city to dwell in;
hungry and thirsty,
    their soul fainted within them.
Then they cried to the LORD in their trouble,
    and he delivered them from their distress.
He led them by a straight way
    till they reached a city to dwell in.
Let them thank the LORD for his steadfast love,
    for his wondrous works to the children of man!
For he satisfies the longing soul,
    and the hungry soul he fills with good things.

PSALM 107:4-9

DISCUSSION QUESTIONS:

What do you think of when you hear the phrase "desert season"? Have you been through a desert season?

What stood out to you about the woman at the well that you may not have thought about before?

In the video, I say, "Your theology is very personal." How do you see that play out in your own life?

What spiritual wells have you gone to in the past to quench your spiritual thirst? Where do you look for fulfillment?

Day One
MARKS OF THE DESERT

READ PSALM 107—ALOUD, IF POSSIBLE.

With which section of the psalm can you most readily identify this time?

Which section is puzzling this time?

Complete the following (v. 4):
Some _____ in _____
_____, finding no _____ to a _____ to
_____ in.

List characteristics of a desert, or "desert wastes."

What type of wandering do you think these people were doing?
Circle the best answer:
sightseeing   aimless   adventurous

One of my favorite pastimes with my youngest is to go "adventuring" on the trails behind our home. Eight miles of hiking and equestrian trials meander through acres upon acres just outside our back gate. The sight of wildflowers blooming according to their season and the sound of wild things scurrying in the underbrush belie the fact that we're smack-dab in the middle of suburbia. Norah and I could wander for hours, marveling at the creativity of the Lord in every web and leaf. This isn't the kind of wandering happening in Psalm 107:4. These poor souls are experiencing an aimless type of wandering. They are searching for a way out but finding none. The landscape is barren and nearly lifeless. They are tired, hungry, and thirsty.

Maybe you haven't found yourself in a physical desert (or maybe you have!), but have you ever felt like an aimless wanderer? Take a moment to describe that season.

There are many marks of a desert season. I want to draw your attention to three characteristics: loneliness, longing, and lament.

LONELINESS

There's alone-ness and then there's loneliness. How would you distinguish the two?

I've found with loneliness I may be utterly surrounded and yet feel completely alone. I desire to make a connection with someone or something but there's an impenetrable wall. I'm ever kept on the outside.

When have you felt lonely? Describe what loneliness has looked like for you.

LONGING

Complete the following from Psalm 107:5:
_____ and _____, their soul _____
within them.

Few longings are as loud as hunger and thirst. Here we are again—desires rising within us. There is nothing wrong with being hungry and thirsty. The Lord fashioned us to need food and water—sustenance outside ourselves. We'll dive into this more deeply on Day Two but for now, know that the desert season is marked by a deep longing to be satisfied and sustained.

A scene in the movie *Three Amigos* aptly depicts the longing in the desert. Lucky, Ned, and Dusty wilt under the heat of the blazing sun. The barren landscape drops behind them as they stop to quench their thirst. The camera pans to Lucky first. He lifts his canteen high above his eager mouth, but only two splashes of water barely wet his tongue. Ned tries next. He isn't as fortunate as Lucky. Something pours from his canteen's spout, but all Ned gets is a mouthful of sand. Last, it's Dusty's turn. Surely his experience will match his amigos'. He longingly raises his canteen and, to the bewilderment of his buddies, water gushes forth. Dusty drinks to his heart's content, gargles and swishes the excess, and drops the canteen to the ground. The remnant soaks into the cracked earth. Once Dusty feels Lucky's and Ned's incredulous stares, he generously offers, "lip balm?"

Does any of that sound familiar? With which amigo do you identify?

Have you felt like you're the only Lucky or Ned in a world full of Dustys? Elaborate.

If you answered yes, may I take this moment to encourage you? You aren't the only one. We all have our share of seasons in the desert. We've known loneliness and longing. More than that, the Lord knows your loneliness and longing. He sees you. He hears you. How do I know this? He's heard me. And before that, He's heard countless others—one of whom He called a man after His own heart—David.

LAMENT

Read Psalm 13. What phrase is repeated in the first two verses of this Psalm? How many times?

How do you feel reading the psalm? What are you thinking? Are you worried for David? Do you wince at him asking the Lord, "how long?"—as if he might be struck down at any moment? Or, are you shaking your head in agreement? Do David's words echo the cry of your own heart? Are there "how" questions you are asking God?

David's heart-cry song has been coined the "howling Psalm."[1] Can you hear it? Howling is a communication device used by wolves to mark territory, but also to connect with the rest of the pack over long distances.[2] David "howls" his plea for deliverance. He feels far from God. He feels forgotten; even worse, he feels as if God is hiding from him. He is stricken with anxiety and his enemy seems to have the upper hand. But, he says in verses 5 and 6:

- -

But I have trusted in your steadfast love; my heart shall rejoice in your salvation. I will sing to the LORD, because he has dealt bountifully with me.

PSALM 13:5-6

- -

In light of our study in Week One, underline words or phrases in the passage above that stand out to you.

Although David felt forgotten, nearly rejected, stricken, and oppressed, he remembered what would anchor him despite the desert. Because he was banking on the Lord's faithful, steadfast love, he was convinced that deliverance would come. He lamented his current condition, but he kept his eye on God's promise to establish his throne forever (2 Sam. 7:16). There is a difference between complaining and lamenting.

Look up the following definitions and record what you find:
Complain:

Lament:

How are the two alike?

How are they different?

Complaining is a shallow response to discomfort. We're more irritated than we are deeply moved. We believe we deserve a better experience than we currently know. Most often when I complain, it's a horizontal act. I sound off to someone who has no control over the situation. I just want to be heard. I just want to complain! Am I alone here?

Lamenting, what David is doing in Psalm 13, is a deep response to real pain. We lament our current condition and long for restoration. We know we don't deserve God's gracious help, but we cry to the Lord to make good on His promise to us. It is a vertical act. We point our faces up like the howling wolf and lift our voices to the only One who is able to deliver us. The complainer seeks comfort while the lamenter seeks the Comforter.

> *If you find yourself in a desert season right now, are you seeking comfort (a reprieve from the conditions) or the Comforter? (Don't answer how you know you "should." Be honest; God already knows.)*

For those of us who cringed at David's "how longs," know this: The Lord welcomes lament. Don't get me wrong, He has a strong rebuke for complaining (see Num. 11:1-3), but He reserved a whole book of the Bible for lamenting. He helps put words in our mouths to pour out our hearts to Him.

Let's close with a prayer from this book of lamenting:

- -

Remember my affliction and my wanderings, the wormwood and the gall! My soul continually remembers it and is bowed down within me. But this I call to mind, and therefore I have hope: The steadfast love of the LORD never ceases; his mercies never come to an end; they are new every morning; great is your faithfulness. "The LORD is my portion," says my soul, "therefore I will hope in him."

LAMENTATIONS 3:19-24

- -

Day Two
BROKEN WELLS

Some of you may roll your eyes at this exercise, but indulge me for a moment. Draw a picture of a well in the first box and an anchor in the next:

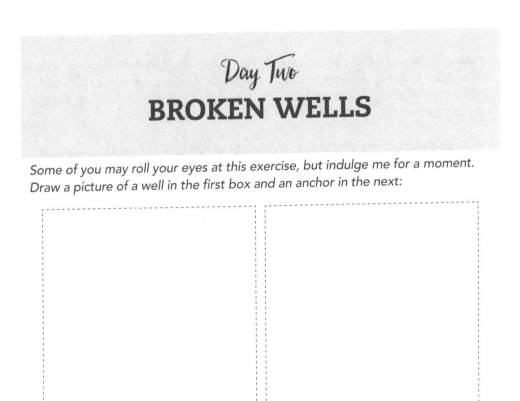

Well   Anchor

Hold on to these two symbols for the rest of our time this week. The lost practice of pen to paper in a digitally-charged world has fostered forgetfulness. Lines and curves made by our hands, no matter how primitive, tend to stick with us.

What is the purpose of a well?

What is the purpose of an anchor?

Although a well and an anchor have two different functions, both are sources. A well is a source of sustenance. It holds water—the most basic need of all humans. An anchor is a source of stability. It holds a vessel fast—keeping it from being swept away by various currents.

Seasons in the desert reveal our wells and anchors—the things in which we find sustenance and stability. To use churchy language, they expose our idols. God used a desert to show His people (the Hebrews) that they trusted more in their oppressors than in the Lord who freed them from oppression.

Read the following passages and give a brief synopsis for each (I've done the first one for you):

Exodus 1:1-6
The Israelites were fruitful, increased rapidly, multiplied, and became extremely numerous so that the land was filled with them.

Exodus 1:8-14

Exodus 2:23-25

Exodus 3:1-10

Exodus 7:1-6

The Lord did what He said He would do. Pharaoh's heart was hardened every time Moses and Aaron approached him concerning the Israelites. Signs and wonders accompanied their requests. Great acts of judgment came against all of Egypt. Ten plagues befell the nation—water turned to blood, frogs, gnats, flies, death of livestock, painful boils, hail, locusts, darkness, and the death of the firstborn. In the final plague, the Lord provided a way of protection for the Israelites. He gave specific instructions regarding what would become a sacred feast for centuries to come (and foreshadow Christ's sacrifice on the cross) called the Passover.

A young, blemish-free lamb was to be killed, its blood painted on the doorposts of their home, its flesh roasted and eaten by the household. Whatever was left over was to be burned. The Lord would pass through the land striking the firstborn of men and beasts but pass over any home painted with the blood. A great mourning broke forth in the land when those not covered by the blood woke to the death of their loved ones. Pharaoh and the Egyptians finally had had enough. They sent the Israelites out of the land in haste. The Lord led them out by way of the Red Sea and the wilderness (or desert) with a pillar of cloud by day and a pillar of fire by night.

Fickle Pharaoh changed his mind about letting them go. He realized the impact his decision would have on Egypt's economy. Not to mention his pride was a bit bruised. Egypt's military might led by Pharaoh himself pursued God's people. When the Israelites encountered the Red Sea ahead and the Egyptian army behind, they cried out to the Lord and Moses, *why did you bring us out here to die?* They continued, *why didn't you just leave us alone in Egypt?* How quickly they changed their tune from, *Lord, deliver us from our oppression,* to, *let us go back to our lives in slavery!* (Proof they were seeking comfort rather than the Comforter.)

Despite their complaining, the Lord parted the Red Sea and invited them to walk on His promise of deliverance. Once every Israelite man, woman, child, and beast stepped out of the dry sea bed, the waters folded back over Pharaoh and the Egyptians who were in hot pursuit.

This was just the beginning. The Lord had much work to do in delivering His people. You see, although the Israelites had been taken out of Egypt, Egypt needed to be taken out of them.

Read Exodus 12:40. How long had the Israelites lived in Egypt?

To give you some perspective, as of this moment, the United States is only 241 years into its nationhood. Generations upon generations of Israelites had called Egypt home. They may have held onto the hope that they would one day be brought out to the land the Lord swore to their forefathers, but Egypt was all they knew. Weaning them from the wells and anchors of Egypt was going to take some time. So, God chose the desert to do so.

Read Deuteronomy 8:2-5. How long were the Israelites in the wilderness?

Before the wilderness/desert, the Israelites had only a vague idea of who God was. Most likely, they looked at Egypt's gods (nearly fifteen hundred of them) to get an idea of who their God might be.[3] The Egyptian gods took the form of every created being—human, animal, or a hybrid of the two. *The Lexham Bible Dictionary* tells us, "it appears that belief in the divine was in some way geared toward gaining control over the natural world as well as protection from dangers within it."[4] Thus, worshipers would give presents, build shelters, and make sacrifices to appease the deities. They would do their part and the gods or goddesses would do theirs. Worship was transactional.

Perhaps the Israelites thought this must be how the LORD, Yahweh, operated. They would do their part to appease the Lord so that they could get what they really wanted—prosperity, progeny, and protection. In His kindness, the Lord obliterated their skewed perception of Yahweh and revealed the broken wells and false anchors in their hearts. The desert proved the Israelites wanted what the Lord could give them more than they wanted Him.

> *Looking again at Deuteronomy 8:2-5, what two goals did God have for His people in the desert?*

> *What does James 4:6 say about the humble?*

> *What is humility?*

> *Deuteronomy 8 says the Lord tested the Israelites to know what was in their hearts, whether or not they would keep His commands. Do you think the Lord already knew what was in their hearts? Do you think they knew?*

Jeremiah 17:9 says, "The heart is deceitful above all things, and desperately sick; who can understand it?" We may think we know our hearts, but according to Jeremiah, they're tricky. Israel may have thought they were doing just fine; all they needed was to shake off the yoke of Egypt. The Lord, who "searches all hearts and understands every plan and thought" (1 Chron. 28:9), knew better. He knows us better too.

We are not unlike Israel. We have notions of who God is that are skewed at best and false at worst. The desert season reveals our broken wells and false anchors—sources of perceived sustenance and stability. He dries up our wells and lets our anchors crumble. He lets us long. He lets us be hungry and thirsty and find no satisfaction in anything but Him.

Don't miss the last line in the Deuteronomy 8 excerpt. The Lord God disciplines His children like a man disciplines his son—out of love and for our good.

Have you found yourself treating God more like a genie in a bottle, rather than a loving Father who wants a relationship? Explain.

What are your broken wells and false anchors—the places you look for sustenance and stability outside of the Lord?

Another term used in the Bible for *well* is *cistern*. The Book of Jeremiah is replete with references to cisterns. They were man-made wells hewn deeply into stone to hold water. When they became defective or useless, they were converted into tombs, torture chambers, and prisons.[5] Jeremiah spoke this against God's people:

- -

... for my people have committed two evils: they have forsaken me, the fountain of living waters, and hewed out cisterns for themselves, broken cisterns that can hold no water.

JEREMIAH 2:13

- -

What do we know happens to broken (defective or useless) cisterns?

Our broken wells will become our prisons. They will dry up, and we'll be left at the bottom trying to figure out how to escape. Our false anchors will fail. We will be swept out to sea—prisoners to the current.

Glance back at Deuteronomy 8:2. Who led the people in the desert?

In His steadfast love, the Lord leads us into the desert, the wilderness, to free us from our faulty wells and anchors. He exposes the desires of our hearts so that we can see them for what they really are. He shows us that we seek comfort more than the Comforter, water for the moment rather than a Fountain whose waters never fail.

Day Three
BETRAYAL

Have you ever felt a "nudge" from the Lord to do something? Maybe it was to send a text to a friend or acquaintance saying, *I'm praying for you today*, or *I'm so grateful for you*; or, perhaps it was to tip a server more generously than usual. Most of the time when I feel those nudges, they're small steps of obedience. I've taken greater leaps of faith concerning decisions that weren't a matter of moral or biblical obedience, more a leaning toward one good thing over another, or one hard thing over another. Rarely, though, have I felt pulled to do something like Hosea did.

Read Hosea 1:2-3. Who spoke to Hosea?

How many times had He spoken to Hosea before this interaction?

What did He tell Hosea to do? Did Hosea do it?

What is Hosea's wife's name? What is the Lord's reason for having him marry her?

Hosea didn't feel a nudge or leaning. Scripture says, "The word of the LORD ... came to [him]" (Hos. 1:1). The means of his calling was appropriate for what he was being asked to do. It was no small thing to knowingly marry someone who would betray him.

Remember when we talked about the significance of names in Week One? The Lord had Hosea give his children the most unusual names. Scan the rest of Hosea 1 to find them. Record each one below.

Doesn't *Not My People* have a ring to it? What was the Lord thinking? Why on earth would He assign these children such depressing names?

The Lord instructed Hosea concerning his wife and children in order to paint a living, breathing picture of the current state of Israel. The children of Israel had fallen into the same traps as their forefathers. The people enjoyed peace and prosperity but then forgot about God. Like Gomer, they had forsaken their first love and gone after cheap substitutes. Because the Lord loves His people and therefore will not tolerate them choosing sloppy seconds, He says this to them:

Therefore I will hedge up her way with thorns, and I will build a wall against her, so that she cannot find her paths. She shall pursue her lovers but not overtake them, and she shall seek them but shall not find them. Then she shall say, "I will go and return to my first husband, for it was better for me then than now." And she did not know that it was I who gave her the grain, the wine, and the oil, and who lavished on her silver and gold, which they used for Baal.

HOSEA 2:6-8

Has it ever seemed like the Lord has hedged up your way with thorns or built a wall against you so that you couldn't find your path? What were you trying to do/achieve/receive?

How did you respond to being hedged up and/or built against?

In my early twenties, all I wanted to do was travel, sing, and write music. It seemed glamorous and fun and what (I thought) the Lord would have for me. Matt (my husband) was an itinerant preacher so I joined him on his trips—from the most obscure west Texas towns to retreats nestled in the Rockies and everywhere in between. We were teamed up with a couple of worship leaders who became lifelong friends. *Here was my chance,* I thought. I could hop up on stage with them, sing my guts out, and fulfill my dreams. The Lord had other plans. Our friends offered me a position with them but it wasn't what I'd hoped. I became their booking agent (and I was THE WORST). I loathe talking on the phone and guess what booking agents do mostly (or did at that time before email was so widely used)? Yep. I was miserable. I remember sitting on a king-size bed in a musty motel room, crying out to the Lord, *Why? Why is it so hard for me? Why does the world seem to be against me? Why do You seem to be against me?*

My way had been hedged up with thorns. And thorns hurt. It didn't seem like I was asking for much, but the Lord loved me too much to let me have what I wanted. As I look back, I can see the "walls" that He built around me were His arms enfolding me. The thorns were less like punishment and more like protection.

My voice, my gifts, my desires were given to me by God just as He gave Israel the grain, new wine, oil, silver, and gold. And just like Israel, I was using His good gifts to serve something or someone else—me. I wanted the glory. I wanted the praise.

> *Are there good gifts He has given you that you are using to serve something or someone else? What are they? Whom or what are they serving?*

I had entered the first desert season I'd ever known. I was lonely, longing for relief, and lamenting where I found myself. The Lord had a plan for me in the middle of my wilderness as He did for Israel, and as He does for you:

- -

> *Therefore, behold, I will allure her, and bring her into the wilderness, and speak tenderly to her. And there I will give her her vineyards and make the Valley of Achor a door of hope. And there she shall answer as in the days of her youth, as at the time when she came out of the land of Egypt. And in that day, declares the LORD, you will call me "My Husband," and no longer will you call me "My Baal." For I will remove the names of the Baals from her mouth, and they shall be remembered by name no more. And I will make for them a covenant*

on that day with the beasts of the field, the birds of the heavens, and the creeping things of the ground. And I will abolish the bow, the sword, and war from the land, and I will make you lie down in safety. And I will betroth you to me forever. I will betroth you to me in righteousness and in justice, in steadfast love and in mercy. I will betroth you to me in faithfulness. And you shall know the LORD.

HOSEA 2:14-20

- -

In the text above, underline where the Lord is leading (alluring) her. Circle where it says He will give her vineyards back.

Underline what she will call the Lord. What had she previously called Him?

Who will she know (last line)?

The Lord would lead His people into the wilderness, the desert, to expose their betrayal and to betroth them to Him in faithfulness forever. He would show them that He wasn't like the Baals (false gods). He didn't need to be appeased or bought. Essentially, He was saying, *let me love you. As a husband should love his wife, let me love you.*

Israel had been seduced by a period of peace and prosperity. They confused the created with the Creator, the gift with the Giver. Broken wells and false anchors were more appealing than Yahweh—I AM WHO I AM. He loved His people too much to let them continue in their betrayal. So, He led them into the desert.

Do you find yourself in the desert? Will you let Him love you there, right where you are?

Day Four
BEARING FRUIT

I'm taking you back to Exodus. I know you thought we were mostly done there, but we're not. I don't think we ever will be. Exodus isn't only the Israelites' story; it's ours too.

Moses was a man for whom God obviously had a plan from the beginning. When Pharaoh ordered all of the Hebrew baby boys to be killed at birth (Ex. 1:16), there were midwives who courageously disobeyed. Moses was one of the boys saved. His mother hid him for three months and then put him in a basket coated with pitch and set it in the reeds along the Nile. His sister kept watch over him from a distance and witnessed Pharaoh's daughter rescue him from the reeds and eventually adopt him as her own. Although Moses grew up in Pharaoh's household, he didn't forget who he was or the people to which he belonged.

Read Exodus 2:11-15. What does it say Moses "went out" to do?

What did he see?

How did he respond?

What did he see on "the next day"?

What did he say to them? And how did they respond?

Flip over to Acts 7:23-25.

- -

When he was forty years old, it came into his heart to visit his brothers, the children of Israel. And seeing one of them being wronged, he defended the oppressed man and avenged him by striking down the Egyptian. He supposed that his brothers would understand that God was giving them salvation by his hand, but they did not understand.

- -

It appears Moses had an inkling of his calling. He knew God had placed him in a certain time and place to deliver His people. What he didn't know was that the Lord had something else in mind for him first. Moses needed to experience his own exodus into the wilderness before he could lead God's people through theirs.

Look at Exodus 2:15. Where did Moses flee? Why?

Beside what did he sit down?

Those wells keep showing up! Remember in Hosea, the Lord would give her vineyards back *there* in the wilderness? He does it again with Moses. He provides for him in the middle of the desert—long before He leads him out. Forty years, to be exact (Acts 7:30).

Read Exodus 3:1-10. Where was Moses and what was he doing?

Whose flock was it?

Who appeared to him, and how?

Who saw Moses?

Who spoke first?

Moses, the adopted grandson of Pharaoh, accustomed to a life of luxury, found himself in "the far side of the wilderness" (CSB) tending a flock that wasn't even his (Ex. 3:1). But it wasn't his voice that called out first in the desert, demanding to fulfill his calling; it was the Lord's. The time had finally come for Moses to lead God's people out of Egypt. Unlike before, it would be in God's perfect timing.

Notice the similarities and the differences:

EXODUS 2:11-14A	EXODUS 3:7-10
One day, when Moses had grown up, he went out to his people and looked on their burdens, and he saw an Egyptian beating a Hebrew, one of his people. 12 He looked this way and that, and seeing no one, he struck down the Egyptian and hid him in the sand. 13 When he went out the next day, behold, two Hebrews were struggling together. And he said to the man in the wrong, "Why do you strike your companion?" 14 He answered, "Who made you a prince and a judge over us? Do you mean to kill me as you killed the Egyptian?"	Then the LORD said, "I have surely seen the affliction of my people who are in Egypt and have heard their cry because of their taskmasters. I know their sufferings, 8 and I have come down to deliver them out of the hand of the Egyptians and to bring them up out of that land to a good and broad land, a land flowing with milk and honey, to the place of the Canaanites, the Hittites, the Amorites, the Perizzites, the Hivites, and the Jebusites. 9 And now, behold, the cry of the people of Israel has come to me, and I have also seen the oppression with which the Egyptians oppress them. 10 Come, I will send you to Pharaoh that you may bring my people, the children of Israel, out of Egypt."

Both Moses and the Lord "saw" the misery of the people. Moses "went out" but the Lord "came down." What does this say about Moses' and the Lord's position in relation to the people?

Before Moses' personal exodus, he took it upon himself to rescue God's people. He didn't realize that he was just as needy as his brothers and sisters. They may have been carrying the actual heavy burdens, but Moses carried the equally heavy burden of pride. Only Someone who had to "come down" to view the people's misery could truly rescue them.

We see the effect forty years in the wilderness had on Moses. What does he say in Exodus 3:11?

From what we know of the rest of the story, does God use Moses to deliver His people from Egypt?

Friend, you may be in the middle of your wilderness/desert because the Lord is preparing you for a new season of ministry. You may know your calling but perhaps you have decided to fulfill it on your terms (like Moses) and made a mess (like Moses).

Can I get an amen? Is this you? Elaborate.

Where do you think you are in the process?
_____ *Forcing the fulfillment*
_____ *Fleeing the consequences*
_____ *Settling into life in the wilderness*
_____ *Humbly accepting God's call*

Seasons in the desert are often used by God to prepare us to bear fruit. He humbles us before the harvest so that we know it's His power and glory, not ours. We see this perfectly displayed in Christ's temptation in the wilderness.

Read Luke 4:1-2. Who led Jesus into the wilderness? For how long and for what reason?

What did He eat while there?

Before we see Jesus in Luke 4, the only public appearance He made was His baptism by John. At His baptism, the Spirit descended like a dove on Jesus and a voice from heaven told the witnesses that He is the Father's beloved Son in whom He delights. The gospel according to Lauren would have looked something like this: *and then Jesus forged ahead, fulfilling Isaiah's prophecy to bring good news to the poor, heal the brokenhearted, free the captives, and proclaim the year of the Lord's favor.* That's not exactly what happened.

Read Luke 4:3-12. Complete the table below:

TEMPTATION	JESUS' RESPONSE
If you are the Son of God, command this stone to become bread.	
To you I will give all this authority and their glory, for it has been delivered to me, and I give it to whom I will. If you, then, will worship me, it will all be yours.	
If you are the Son of God, throw yourself down from here, for it is written, "He will command his angels concerning you, to guard you," and "On their hands they will bear you up, lest you strike your foot against a stone."	

The devil has no new ideas. He comes after Christ the way he came after Eve. He appeals to Jesus' human desires—hunger, power, glory, and protection—in hopes of drawing Him away from His task on earth. What's His task? He came, not to condemn, but to save the world (John 3:16-17).

Jesus not only died for us, He lived for us too. Fully man and fully God, He obeyed God the Father perfectly. In all the ways Adam and Eve failed when they faced the serpent, Jesus succeeded. When we believe in Christ—that His life and death are enough for us—it's as if His life is laid on top of ours and all God the Father sees is Jesus' perfect obedience.

Satan attempted to sabotage God's plan to save sinners. He attacked Jesus' identity ("IF you are the Son of God ..."). He tempted Him to take matters into His own hands ("command this stone to become bread") to satisfy a very real desire (hunger). He tempted Him to forsake God the Father and go after power and glory outside of the Father's plan. When Jesus fought back with Scripture, Satan followed suit but twisting the truth to serve his purposes. Jesus would not be deterred. He faithfully and humbly prevailed.

The NIV translates Luke 4:13 this way:

> *When the devil had finished all this tempting,*
> *he left him* **until an opportune time**.

LUKE 4:13 (emphasis mine)

Here's what we can be sure of: Satan will take advantage of our desert seasons simply because they are "opportune times." The desert is wild and makes us vulnerable. Take heart, friend, the Lord is working in the wilderness. Although it may feel like it, He has not left us. He very well might be preparing us for a season of bearing glorious fruit. And when we fall to temptation, if we believe in Christ, His obedience is enough for us. We get to confess our failure, brush ourselves off, and turn back to Him. What a relief!

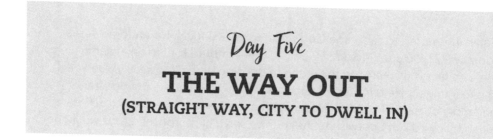

Day Five

THE WAY OUT
(STRAIGHT WAY, CITY TO DWELL IN)

Let's begin today with a little status update.

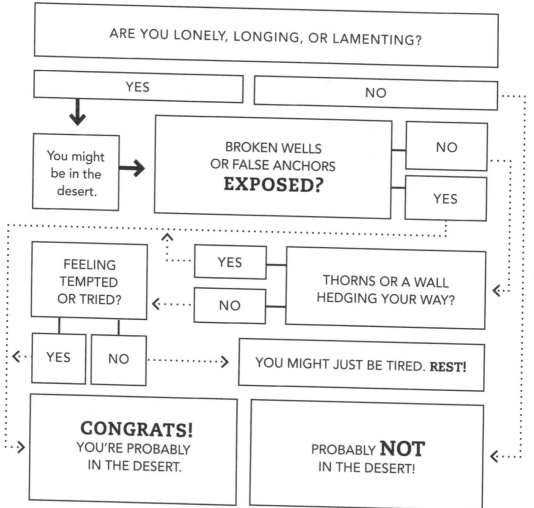

IN THE DESERT?

ARE YOU LONELY, LONGING, OR LAMENTING?

YES | NO

You might be in the desert.

BROKEN WELLS OR FALSE ANCHORS **EXPOSED?**

NO | YES

FEELING TEMPTED OR TRIED?

YES | NO

THORNS OR A WALL HEDGING YOUR WAY?

YES | NO

YOU MIGHT JUST BE TIRED. **REST!**

CONGRATS! YOU'RE PROBABLY IN THE DESERT.

PROBABLY **NOT** IN THE DESERT!

Now that we've determined your (probable) status, if you're in the desert, how do you get out?

Let's start with the good news.

In most of the scenarios set forth this week—the Israelites coming out of Egypt, Hosea, Jesus' temptation—who led them into the desert?

If the Lord has led you into the desert, He is the only One who can lead you out. He alone knows the way. In our own strength, we'll wander until we waste away; but with His steadfast love, He will lead us out.

Some wandered in desert wastes, finding no way to a city to dwell in; hungry and thirsty, their soul fainted within them. Then they cried to the LORD in their trouble, and he delivered them from their distress. He led them by a straight way till they reached a city to dwell in. Let them thank the LORD for his steadfast love, for his wondrous works to the children of man! For he satisfies the longing soul, and the hungry soul he fills with good things.

PSALM 107:4-9

Looking at the text above, what did the people do first?

Where does it say they were when they cried out?

POOR AND NEEDY

In order to cry out, we have to first realize that we are not okay. We are poor, needy, and cannot find our own way out. Admitting we're poor and needy isn't always comfortable. I'll be the first to say that I don't like being labeled "needy."

I'd rather be the one who has it all together. In God's economy, it's not the rich and powerful who get His attention but the poor and needy.

Summarize the following verses:
Psalm 40:17

Psalm 72:12-13

Isaiah 41:17-18

Have you come to the place where you recognize that you are not okay? Explain.

My husband repeats this phrase at our church at least once a month, "It's okay to not be okay. You just can't stay there." You may recognize that you're not okay, but are you willing to be led out of the desert?

STRAIGHT WAY

In the CSB version of Psalm 107:7, it says the Lord led them by the "right path." In the ESV, it translates that phrase as "straight way." The Hebrew word for the adjective means both and a few more: stretched,[6] right, straight, level, smooth.[7] I want to latch onto "straight" for now.

Think back to the beginning of the week. What were the people in Psalm 107 doing in the desert?

This straight way is not like the aimless wandering the people were experiencing at first. There is a destination. We'll get to that in a minute. For now, let's keep looking at the straight way.

Read Hebrews 12:12-13. See anything familiar? If so, what?

I'll give you some context to these verses. The chapter before (Heb. 11) has been dubbed the "hall of faith." The author of Hebrews lists men and women who were commended for their faith. In other words, they believed God was who He said He was and would do what He said He would do. They trusted Him even when they couldn't see the end, even when it cost them pain and suffering. Chapter 12 starts as an encouragement to the rest of us—those who get to exercise the same kind of faith. We are exhorted to throw off the extra baggage of sin and other hindrances to running our race well and to keep our eyes on Jesus, the Beginner and Finisher of our faith. We are reminded that the Lord disciplines those whom He loves, just as a loving father disciplines his children. In light of this, we are encouraged to make "straight paths" for our feet so that what is lame may not be dislocated but rather healed.

> *As we admit we're not okay and seek to be led out of the desert, we can follow in a way that's helpful or in a way that's careless. The admonition to make straight paths for our feet is for our good. What does it mean though?*

Step carefully. Don't dig potholes for yourself. Pay attention to what keeps your focus on Jesus.

I'll borrow from my husband again (he doesn't mind). There's a thing he calls a "Stir and Steals List." This is a list of all the things that stir our affections for Jesus and the things that steal our affections for Jesus. For our trip out of the desert, we could rename these "straight path" and "potholes."

For me, I would list spending time in the Word as a "stir/straight path." It doesn't have to be as obvious as that; for example, spending time in nature is another "stir." Too much time on social media is a "steal/pothole" for me. These won't look the same from person to person. Some of you may have no problem spending time on social media. That may not be a "steal" for you, while for others it might be.

Think for a little bit about what "stirs" and "steals" your affections for Jesus. You may even want to come back to this page throughout the study to add to or edit the list. But go ahead and get started here:

STIRS/STRAIGHT PATH	STEALS/POTHOLES

Before we move on to the destination, let's take a look at the noun being modified by the adjective (straight) in Psalm 107:7.

A straight _____.

The Lord will lead us out of the desert but it's still a journey. He could teleport wherever He wants (and sometimes He does), but most often, He takes His time. Why? Because He is building endurance within us.

Endurance is something He values and it's something He does well.

Note what you find about endurance in the verses below:
Romans 5:4

Romans 15:5

Hebrews 12:1

Revelation 2:2,19; 3:10

As a runner, I have learned there is no way to build endurance except to put in the miles. The same is true with spiritual endurance. He will build it in us as we journey with Him.

Have you seen God building endurance in your life? If so, how?

A CITY TO DWELL IN

The wilderness is a wild and uninhabitable land. We are not meant to stay there. The Lord is bringing us to "a city to dwell in."

Matt and I bought a little patch of land only a mile or so from the hustle and bustle of town. We wanted more peace and quiet in a pastoral setting. We're not alone. Most conversations with friends about their dreams for a home center around having a little bit more land, being out from town, and having room to breathe and play. To us, the notion of a city is the opposite of rest, but for those wandering the desert, a city would be the one place they could finally rest.

What does Exodus 20:8-11 say about rest? (Hint: the Sabbath is a day of rest and worship.)

Do you think God needed to rest? Explain.

The Lord built us to rest and He showed us how to do it: work hard six days and on the seventh, rest. This resting reminds us that we can't do it all. We have to depend on the Lord—His breath in our lungs, His sustaining grace in our lives, and His work on our behalf through Jesus' life, death, and resurrection.

Are there ways the Lord is inviting you to rest that you are refusing? If so, name them. And if you're tired of refusing, write a prayer of surrender.

A key component to being able to rest is to feel protected. When we're out in the desert, rest is hard to come by because we are open to the elements. We feel exposed and vulnerable. There are no walls to protect us—no sturdy structure within which to find refuge.

Cities in the ancient world were surrounded by great walls to protect the people and the property within them. They had to be built high enough and thick enough to withstand attacks from neighboring nations.

Psalm 27 reminds us that God is the stronghold of our lives. What do you think this means in light of Romans 8:28,31-35,38-39?

The city is full of people of all sizes, shapes, and types. When the Lord leads us out of the desert, He leads us into community. We don't have to be alone. We have a family—brothers and sisters in Christ who know us, walk with us. They know what it's like to be in the desert and to be welcomed back. They help put flesh on what we cannot see—becoming the hands and feet of Christ.

How have you seen the people of God be the hands and feet of God for you?

Congratulations—you made it through Week Two! This was no small feat. We covered a lot of ground! I am praying the Lord plants His Word deeply into your heart and that if you currently find yourself in a desert season, there is light at the end of the tunnel. I pray this may even be a little oasis—a place to sit and rest and remember that His steadfast love will never wear out.

Week Three

CHAINS

Some sat in darkness and in the shadow of death,

    prisoners in affliction and in irons,

for they had rebelled against the words of God,

    and spurned the counsel of the Most High.

So he bowed their hearts down with hard labor;

    they fell down, with none to help.

Then they cried to the LORD in their trouble,

    and he delivered them from their distress.

He brought them out of darkness and the shadow of death,

    and burst their bonds apart.

Let them thank the LORD for his steadfast love,

    for his wondrous works to the children of man!

For he shatters the doors of bronze

    and cuts in two the bars of iron.

PSALM 107:10-16

DISCUSSION QUESTIONS:

Read Luke 1:76-79 as a group. How have you seen Jesus fulfill this prophecy to shine a light in the darkness in your own life or in the lives of those you know?

If you don't mind sharing, tell the group about a time when you thought "If this happens, then I will be fulfilled."

What would change in your life if you were to surrender your chains to Christ? How can you follow through on that this week?

Day One
HEAVY

READ PSALM 107—ALOUD, IF POSSIBLE.

With which section of the psalm can you most readily identify this time?

Which section is puzzling this time?

Complete the following from Psalm 107:10-11:

Some sat in darkness and in the shadow of death, _____ in
_____ and in irons, _____ they _____ _____ against
the words of God, and _____ the counsel of the Most High.

I'm usually the optimist, but on this occasion I want to start with the bad news.
Trust me, it can only get better.

Read Romans 3:10-18.

How many are righteous?

How many understand?

How many seek God?

How many have turned aside?

News flash: we are all born with chains. We are enslaved to sin because we are all Adam's offspring. Remember back in Eden (Week One) when Adam and Eve broke the only rule of the garden? That's where it all started.

Eugene H. Peterson (author of *The Message*) put Romans 5:12-14a this way:

> You know the story of how Adam landed us in the dilemma we're in—first sin, then death, and no one exempt from either sin or death. That sin disturbed relations with God in everything and everyone, but the extent of the disturbance was not clear until God spelled it out in detail to Moses. So death, this huge abyss separating us from God, dominated the landscape from Adam to Moses. Even those who didn't sin precisely as Adam did by disobeying a specific command of God still had to experience this termination of life, this separation from God.

Who is exempt from sin and death?

What does it say sin did?

How was it "spelled out in detail to Moses"?

Now turn to Ephesians 2:1-3. Rewrite the passage below in your own words.

Apart from Jesus, we are the walking dead. We look alive but we are trudging through life, driven by primitive appetites. We want what we want when we want it. And thanks to Adam and Eve, we are born with our "wants" broken. We are chained to the desire for false anchors and broken wells.

What's worse is that keeping the law can't break the chains; it only exposes them. We can't keep the law. Even if we tried to, we would attempt only to save ourselves and find salvation outside of the Lord.

Read further down, in Ephesians 2:4-10. (This is where the good news starts!)

How is one saved?

Why are we saved in this manner?

Have you ever come to the place where you recognized that you were powerless to save yourself? Explain.

Jesus came to save those who wear the heavy chains of sin—you and me. He is the only One who could do it. Only He could keep the law perfectly. Being both God and man, born of a virgin and conceived by the Holy Spirit, Adam's sin was not passed on to Him. He had a human nature but not a sin nature. He didn't wear the chains of sin and rebellion like we do.

Have you ever accepted Jesus' rescue? Tell the story below.

Just because some of us have accepted Jesus' rescue, doesn't mean we don't try to put those chains right back on. We might not be owned by Adam's sin any more, but we are owned by something else.

Remember in last week's homework when we were making "straight paths for our feet"? If you look back to the beginning of Hebrews 12, you'll see what I'm talking about.

Read Hebrews 12:1. What are we to lay aside?

The author of Hebrews, in this verse, is addressing runners already in the race. In other words, these aren't the walking dead—those still wearing Adam's chains. These are runners who have already trusted in Jesus' rescue. Something is weighing them down and tripping them up.

If you're feeling weighed down and tripped up but have already shed the Adam-chains, let's do a little diagnostic.

Have you been hurt in a way that still affects how you live today? If so, write a brief summary of what happened and how it affects you now. Feel free to use abbreviations and "code" for your privacy (or don't write it here at all, but maybe write it somewhere and throw it away/burn it later).

Are you "hooked" on someone or something? Does the thought of losing whatever or whomever it is give you an anxiety attack? If so, what or who is it? (Again, feel free to use abbreviations and code words.)

Are you hung up in sin you just can't shake no matter how hard you try? If so, do your best to name it.

Close this time with a prayer of confession to the Lord. Confess where you are. It doesn't have to be pretty or put together. Be honest. Confess what you think your chains might be—Adam's chains, or chains due to a hurt or something on which you're hooked or hung up.

Day Two
HURT, HOOKED, AND HUNG UP

Let's take a look at those things that weigh us down and trip us up.

HURT

- -

Like most things, there is a spectrum of hurt. There's a difference between the pain we feel when we stub our toe versus when we break our femur. Likewise, there's a difference between the pain we feel when we're slighted by an acquaintance or abused by someone we love.

If you answered "yes" to the question at the end of yesterday's homework about a hurt you're still carrying, place an "x" on the following pain scale where it applies:

No Pain   Moderate Pain   Worst Pain

1   2   3   4   5   6   7   8   9   10

Although the initial hurt may vary in its magnitude from one person to another, its effect doesn't necessarily reflect the intensity of the wound. Even a slight wound can fester into a life-threatening infection.

Look up the following passages and note what each says about the Lord and our pain:
Psalm 56:8

Hebrews 4:14-15

Our hurt is not unknown to the Lord. Not only does He keep record of it, He understands it intimately. Jesus, the Son of God, knew what it meant to be wounded.

Record what kind of hurt Jesus suffered in each passage:
Matthew 26:47-49

Matthew 26:69-75

Matthew 27:15-23

Matthew 27:27-31

Matthew 27:33-44

Jesus was verbally and physically abused. He suffered rejection. He was betrayed and denied by those closest to Him. Place a mark by the section of Scripture above with which you most identify.

How did Jesus respond to His abusers and friends who wounded Him?

I think I can safely assume that nearly all of us who have been hurt didn't die for those who hurt us (especially since you have enough breath in your lungs to do a Bible study). It is possible, though, that like Jesus we have forgiven those who hurt us. Usually, that's a process. Our first, most human response tends toward one of two ways: we play the tape of the offense over and over again in our minds, or we pretend the offense never happened.

When you've been hurt, which response is most likely for you?
Circle your answer:

              play the tape   *pretend it never happened*

These responses may be linked to our personality differences. In a fight-or-flight scenario, you may be a fighter. You might play the tape—envisioning how you might have done it differently, how you would have defended yourself, or how to punish your offender. No matter the reason for playing the tape, you dwell on the offense, keeping it fresh, and thus suffering its effects repeatedly as if for the first time. In doing so, the only person punished is you.

Perhaps you more often take flight. You'd rather deny anything ever happened. You flee the hurt. You bury it deep into your consciousness because you don't want to give it power. Surely, you tell yourself, I can overcome this alone. No one needs to know.

Hurt is like a seed planted deep within the earth, it breaks through the hardened crust of our hearts. When we dwell on it, we water and feed it so that it bears bitter fruit in our lives. When we deny it, it's a weed running rampant, choking out even the good. It doesn't need much water to thrive—just a shower or two—moments that remind us of the hurt that we try to push back down.

If you're still suffering from a wound, have you dwelled on or denied the offense? How has that seed sprouted in your life—bearing bitter fruit or becoming an invasive weed? Describe its effect in your life.

Note: If you are experiencing physical or emotional abuse, get safe and get help. I've included resources in the Leader Guide to help you do that.

HOOKED

Sometimes it's not a hurt that "owns" us but a substance or relationship. On Day One, I asked if there was something in your life that the thought of losing launched you into an anxiety attack. Let me make myself clear first: There's nothing wrong with fearing the loss of a loved one. That is completely natural. In fact, if you didn't fear the loss at some level, then I would question the health of your heart! Maybe you're self-protecting so much that you can't feel the most basic (albeit complicated) emotions of affection and love. If this is the case, in the margin, pen a prayer to God asking Him to help you feel. It's a scary prayer, but it's worth it. Even if you trust the Lord to sustain you in the loss, there should be a part of you that aches at the thought.

The fear of a loss can become like chains on our hearts when the thought is all-consuming (you think about it and fear it constantly) and/or when the fear affects your day-to-day life (you order your life or those in your life in a way to protect against any loss). For example, this is more than making your kids wear their seat belts at all times (basic, normal, healthy); it's helicopter-mom on steroids—not letting your kids out of your sight, ever.

Another indicator of a hooked relationship is one that dominates your heart and mind space—one that is more like an obsession. We may say it's love, but it's an imitation.

Read 1 Corinthians 13:4-7. What does this passage say love looks like?

No one will live this perfectly. Only Jesus could and did. But the Lord does give us a picture for which we can aim. It's a love that isn't self-centered, nor is it other-centered. It is God-centered.

If a relationship in your life—romantic or platonic—has come to mind, is it mostly centered on God, on yourself, or the other person?

How does this relationship measure up to 1 Corinthians 13:4-7? Rank it on a scale of 1-10. (1 = not even in the same universe; 10 = as close as humanly possible.)

| 1 | 2 | 3 | 4 | 5 | 6 | 7 | 8 | 9 | 10 |

Maybe it's not a relationship that owns you but a substance. Just because you're going through a Bible study doesn't mean you aren't struggling with an addiction. In fact, you could've picked this study up because of your addiction. If that's you, I am so glad you did! You don't have to live enslaved to a substance. I have included some resources in the Leader Guide to help you find freedom.

Summarize the following verses:
1 Corinthians 6:12

Philippians 3:19

2 Peter 2:19

Is there anything in your life (a relationship, substance, experience, object) that dominates you, is driven by your appetite, or overcomes you? Something that you would go through "withdrawal" to give up for a season?

HUNG UP

I've had seasons of being owned by a hurt and being hooked, but by far I've seen the Lord work the most in the places I have been hung up in sin. My sin didn't look so bad. These chains were more like jewelry than shackles. Still, they enslaved me.

I wanted to be perfect. I wanted to get everything right. Basically, I didn't want to need God. On top of that, I wanted praise for my perfection. To be perfect wasn't enough. I wanted the admiration that comes with it. I had a goal in mind for myself—a point I wanted to achieve—a finish line. I said to myself, if _____, then I'll know I'm good enough.

Have you ever had these thoughts? Explain.

What would your blanks look like?

If _____, then I'll know
_____.

Here are some examples:

If we buy that house, then I'll be happy.
If I have that car, then I'll feel fulfilled.
If I'm invited to their party, then I'll feel accepted.
If they accept me, then I'll know I'm good enough.
If I were married, then I'd know I'm desirable.
If I lost this weight, then I'd be worthy.

How has that turned out for you? Have the thens of those statements panned out? If so, how long did that last?

Do you struggle with perfectionism? Do you always want to get it right, be the best, achieve the most?

Friend, welcome to the spiritual treadmill. You run for hours and hours, miles upon miles but never get anywhere. You are right where you started. The finish line is ever moving. Perfection is impossible for human beings. The only perfection we can attain is that which has already been given to us by Jesus.

What does Hebrews 12:2 call Jesus?

We will continue to further expose our chains this week. Don't let this overwhelm or discourage you. The Lord is working! He delights to shine light on our chains so that we may break free!

Write 2 Corinthians 12:9 below. Ask the Lord to help you believe what it says.

Day Three
GOD MOST HIGH

Turn to Psalm 107:10-11 and answer the following questions:
By what name is God referred to here?

The Hebrew word for this name is El Elyon. It occurs the most in the Psalms and the Book of Daniel.[1] I've pulled a few verses for you to read and note what you find about the Most High:

Psalm 18:13

Psalm 21:7

Psalm 47:2

Psalm 83:18

Daniel 4:17

Daniel 7:27

What is a common theme in these verses? Circle the best answer:

God as Shepherd   God as Most High King   God as Light

According to these texts, what or who is higher than the Most High?

You got it. Nothing and no one is higher than the Most High. He is the King who gives the kings of earth their power and dominion. He is ultimately higher and more powerful than anything in the heavens or on earth. His position as Most High has bearing on perspective and power.

PERSPECTIVE

What does Isaiah 55:9 say about God's ways and thoughts?

Imagine you're stuck in traffic in a congested, downtown area. Skyscrapers tower over every intersection. Your navigation device with traffic alerts is on the fritz so you can only trust what you can see—cars on all sides. However, you have a friend working on the ninetieth floor of a building two blocks away.

Whose position gives the best perspective in this situation?

Keep using your imagination: You see what looks like a way out—an alley to your right, clear of traffic. Your friend sees it too, but she can also see that the shortcut is actually the quickest route to a dead end.

God, being Most High, has the best perspective on life and flourishing. After all, He is also Creator and Sustainer of it. I like how Wayne Grudem, in his book *Christian Beliefs*, describes God's knowledge:

> Since he fully knows himself (1 Cor. 2:10-11), he fully knows all things that he could have done but did not do and all things that he might have created but did not create. He also knows all possible events that will not actually happen, and events that would have resulted if some other events had turned out differently in history (see, for example, Matt. 11:21).[2]

Let's get personal. Based on what we've uncovered about the Lord being Most High, who has a better perspective on your life, you or God?

The problem with knowing something in our heads is that it doesn't necessarily mean we show it with our lives.

Would you say you live in such a way that proves you believe God has the best perspective on your life?

POWER

What does Psalm 115:3 say about God's power?

In Daniel 4, we find a strange story that tells of God's High-ness in regard to His power. King Nebuchadnezzar had a frightening dream and called in all the magicians and diviners to interpret it for him. None of them could interpret it, so he called in Daniel (also known as Belteshazzar) to interpret it for him.

Read about the dream in verses 13-18. Then read Daniel's response in verses 20-27.

What did Daniel tell the king to do? Before reading further, do you think Nebuchadnezzar did what Daniel advised?

Check out what happened in verses 29-33. What was the problem with the king's response to his dream?

What lesson do you think God wanted him to learn (see vv. 34-37)?

Complete Nebuchadnezzar's response in verses 34b-35:

... for his _____ is an everlasting dominion,
and his _____ endures from generation to generation;
all the inhabitants of the earth are accounted as nothing,
and he _____ according to _____ _____ among the host of
heaven and among the inhabitants of the earth;
and _____ can _____ his hand
or say to him, "_____ _____ _____ _____?"

Have you ever found yourself asking the Lord, "What have You done?" (It's okay; He already knows the answer.)

King Nebuchadnezzar's problem was that he thought all the wealth and blessing of his kingdom was a result of his rule. He felt in control of his own destiny and his kingdom's destiny. The Lord showed him the truth. He humbled him for his own good.

Think back to yesterday's homework—the hurt, or the thing on which you're hooked or hung up. Holding on to those things is essentially a refusal to release them to the Most High. It's a desire to be in control. We make vows that will never last.

> *Place a mark by the vow(s) you are tempted to make:*
> ☐ *I will never be hurt again.*
> ☐ *I will never know happiness without this one thing.*
> ☐ *I will get it right.*
> *How is that working for you? Have you managed to keep the vow(s)?*

None of us can keep the vows we've made. We don't have the perspective and the power of the Most High. And, as I've pointed out, even if we recognize we don't have the perspective and power and we credit God as Most High, our lives don't match up to what we know. Knowing isn't believing and trusting.

Maybe you're not so sure about God Most High. He sounds terrifying and kind of mean. You think, why would I trust a God who might turn me into a cow? There's good news, I promise. As people living on this side of Christ's first coming, we get to see undisputed evidence of the steadfast love of God in Jesus.

> *Write an honest prayer to God Most High. Confess your vow(s) and your hesitation in trusting Him, and lift your chains up to Him. Recognize that He alone has ultimate perspective and power.*

Day Four
SLAVES TO SONS

Yesterday, we studied the name the psalmist uses in Psalm 107:11 to address God. What name was it?

Before we move on, I want to dig a bit further in Scripture for more occurrences of that name. In the New Testament, Jesus is referred to as Son of the Most High in the following verses. Write down who calls Him by that name:

Mark 5:7-9

Luke 1:26-33

What is the relationship between Jesus and the ones who call Him by that name?

Read Acts 16:17-18. Is what the slave girl with the spirit of divination said true?

These verses are sobering. James 2:19 says that "even the demons believe—and shudder!" We can have an accurate view of God (and an appropriate response!) without a personal relationship with Him. And, yes, the angels are personal messengers of God Most High but their relationship is more like that of a general and his inferiors and less like a father and a son. As creatures made in His image, we are set apart from the rest of creation. We are invited to be more than servants. In Christ, we are welcomed as sons and daughters. More on that later.

For now, I like what Eugene Peterson has to say about knowing God:

We do not know God by defining him but by
being loved by him and loving in return.[3]

Do you feel like you know more about God than you know Him?

BOWED HEARTS

Let's turn our attention back to Psalm 107, specifically verse 12. What do you think is meant by "he bowed their hearts down"?

Why do you think they needed their hearts bowed down?

When we are hurt, hooked, or hung up and trying our hardest to exert control, we are essentially believing that we are higher than God. Our hearts are exalting ourselves above Him. They are proud and in the wrong place, needing to be humbled because we are not the Most High. We don't have the best perspective nor the power to really do anything about anything. It is loving and merciful of God to put us in our place because we wreck it all.

Does this resonate with you? Are you at a place where your heart feels "bowed down"? If so, what circumstances brought about your bowed heart?

This heart bowed down thing isn't easy. It's hard and heavy. It can feel as if your heart is physically flopped over itself—the heart working extra hard to pump blood through, labored breath with each beat. You feel like you've tried everything to free the chains, deal with the hurt, throw off the hooks, untangle yourself from the hang-up. Nothing has worked. Welcome to a bowed heart.

HARD LABOR

Take a trip back with me to peek in at the Israelites in Egypt before the Lord delivered them. Read the following verses and write a brief summary of each selection. I've included icons to help you along the way.

Exodus 2:23-25

Exodus 3:1-2,7-10

Exodus 4:1-17

Exodus 4:27-31

Exodus 5:1-9

I want to draw your attention to one verse in particular, Exodus 4:31:

And the people believed; and when they heard that the Lord had visited the people of Israel and that he had seen their affliction, they bowed their heads and worshiped.

What did the people bow in response to their cries being heard?

Here's the reality: We don't even know the state of our own hearts. We may think that our hearts are bowed down because our heads are but that isn't necessarily the case. The Lord knows though. Since He loves us and knows what's best for us, He will make sure our hearts are in a place to receive His deliverance. Think about it this way: if the Lord had simply rescued the Israelites from Egypt the first moment they cried out, when they hit the hard of the wilderness, Egypt wouldn't have looked so bad. They might have wanted to go back to Egypt. In fact, they did just that (see Ex. 14:12; Num. 11:4-6;14:1-4). Even after their burdens were laid on heavier, the Israelites longed to return to the familiarity of Egypt! Imagine if they had barely suffered?

Isn't that like us? Sometimes it takes rock bottom for us to finally look up for rescue. Sometimes it takes a heart bowed down with hard labor to wake us up to our chains. In His steadfast love, He will make that hurt sting. He will press His eternally powerful finger on that wound to show He's not done there. He will let us suffer the consequences of that substance or relationship. He will let us grow tired and weary of trying to get it right in our own strength.

Has the Lord used "hard labor" to bow your heart down? What has that looked like in your life?

SLAVES TO THE LAW

Without Christ, we are slaves to our chains—those false anchors and dry wells that have become prisons. We can try to break out but our efforts will be fruitless.

Read Galatians 4:3-7 and answer the following:
What were we enslaved to?

What do you think it means by "under the law"? (Hint: look back at Day One's homework this week.)

Who redeemed us?

What did we receive in addition to redemption?

What did God send into our hearts?

What do we get to call God now?

SONS BY THE SPIRIT

Throughout the New Testament, we are reminded that we are made sons and daughters of God through Christ's redemption.

Put the following verses in your own words:
John 1:12-13

Romans 8:1-5

Galatians 3:26

1 John 3:1-2

Conclude today by giving thanks to the Father for redemption, for freedom from our chains, for the right to be called sons and daughters of God.

Day Five
OUT OF DARKNESS

In our old house, we had something akin to the standard vanity bar for lighting in our master bathroom. Although it provided adequate light, it left something to be desired aesthetically. One fault (among many) in my life, is that I will choose pretty over practical. This was the case when I decided to replace the drab vanity bar with a more updated fixture.

Our handyman friend, Ron, installed the new light for us, and I couldn't wait to see it hanging above the mirror. Unfortunately, there was little to no natural light in our bathroom already and the light fixture barely helped. I could hardly see a thing! I was too hardheaded to admit that I had made a mistake, so we kept that light until the day we sold the house. The problem with the ineffective light fixture is that the dark can hide all kinds of ugly. Who knows what my makeup looked like in the light of day!

In this excerpt from Psalm 107, underline or circle each reference to the dark:

Some sat in darkness and in the shadow of death,
prisoners in affliction and in irons,
for they had rebelled against the words of God,
and spurned the counsel of the Most High.
So he bowed their hearts down with hard labor;
they fell down, with none to help.
Then they cried to the LORD in their trouble,
and he delivered them from their distress.
He brought them out of darkness and the shadow of death,
and burst their bonds apart.

PSALM 107:10-14

FROM DARKNESS TO LIGHT

Colossians 1:12-14 connects our adoption out of slavery and into being sons and daughters to being brought out of darkness and the shadow of death. Complete the following:

... giving thanks to the _____, who has qualified you to share in the _____ of the saints in _____. He has delivered us from the domain of _____ and transferred us to the _____ of his beloved _____, in whom we have _____, the _____ of _____.

Who has qualified us?

What are we qualified to share?

Who delivered us?

Who is the active agent and who is the passive party?

The Greek word for *delivered* (go ahead and circle it in the passage above) is *rhyomai*.[4] Read what this commentary says about Paul (the writer of Colossians) choosing that word here in Colossians 1:13:

The verb translated *rescue* (*rhyomai*) echoes the Old Testament stories of God's intervention to deliver an embattled Israel from its enemies, especially the master story of the exodus, when God delivered Israel from the pharaoh's tyranny ... [5]

Pretty cool, huh? Paul, under the inspiration of the Holy Spirit, shows that God is still doing the same kinds of things that He did back when He led the Israelites out of Egypt—bowed hearts, hard labor, slaves to sons, and now, out of darkness into light.

What do you think is the "domain of darkness"?

The domain of darkness is just as cosmic and otherworldly as it sounds. There are two parts to the darkness: the demonic realm and our darkened minds outside of Christ. Ephesians 6:12 tells us that we wrestle not against flesh and blood, but against the rulers, authorities, the cosmic powers over this present darkness, and the spiritual forces of evil in the heavenly places. Earlier in Ephesians (chapter 4 to be exact), Paul urges believers in Christ not to walk through life like unbelievers—darkened in their minds because of their hardened hearts, enslaved, addicted, striving in their own strength, and living as if God didn't exist.

For those who have not trusted Christ as their Savior, there is only darkness. But for those who have trusted Christ, although we have been rescued from the domain of darkness—the rule of the enemy and the hardness of our hearts because of sin—and have been transferred to the kingdom of Christ, we can slip our wrists back through the chains and sit in the darkness and shadows of our own prisons—the false anchors and broken wells.

Have you felt the darkness and shadows while in your chains? Has it been hard to see?

EXPOSED

Here's the good news: Light always drowns out the dark. You can't be in a light room and turn on the dark. It's impossible.

Read 1 John 1:5-8.
What is being said about God here (v. 5)?

What does it say about us if we claim to walk with God but still walk in darkness?

What happens when we walk in the light?

What consolation is offered here?

Do we have to get "cleaned up" before we walk in the light? Explain.

The beauty of 1 John 1:5-8 is that it calls everyone out. No one is let off the hook. Each one of us struggles with sin and will continue to struggle against the false anchors and broken wells until Christ's return. God knows this. It isn't a surprise to Him. He welcomes us to walk in the light, confess our sins, and be welcomed into community with Him and fellow believers. Here's the deal, though, walking in the light after our eyes have adjusted to the dark is a bit terrifying and disorienting. Remember, the dark hides all kinds of ugly. We will be confronted with our sin and the destruction it has caused to ourselves and others. Oh, but friend, it is worth it! We don't have to be alone in our chains any more—we get to have true fellowship with the Lord and others! We bring the ugly into the light so that we can finally deal with it!

Has the light been terrifying for you?

What has it uncovered in you?

When the Lord shines His light in our darkness, it exposes but it also illuminates. The Lord's forgiveness and Christ's righteousness cover us like the most brilliant robe. God does not uncover to shame us but to further cover us with His grace, love, righteousness, and glory.

MADE ALIVE

Read Psalm 107:14 again.

Apart from Christ, we are all dead in our trespasses and sins (our addiction to false anchors and broken wells). When we accept Christ's rescue—His perfect life for ours, His death on the cross, resurrection from the dead, and ascension to the Father—He makes us truly alive (Eph. 2:5). What can happen though, even to the believer, is we can return to our chains and act like the walking dead. We use our chains to numb ourselves to pain or to help us feel some kind of control.

When we bring our chains into the light and forsake our wells and anchors, we start acting like the walking living that we are. However, with life comes feeling because dead things don't feel. And when we feel, we have all the feels. We don't get to choose only feeling pleasure and never the pain. We will experience both. Just like the light, this is terrifying at first.

The hurt might get worse before it gets better. Letting go of that relationship or substance will feel like death. Recognizing that you will never "get it right" on your own will be crushing.

But the Lord of steadfast love will ...

- ... begin His healing work on the wound;

- ... be a better Father and Lover of your soul than the harsh master of your addiction;

- ... lavish His grace upon you: for His grace is sufficient for us, for His power is made perfect in weakness (2 Cor. 12:9).

In bringing your chains to light, has the pain increased? How?

Do any of the above statements hit a nerve with you? Which one(s)?

DEMO DAY

In most home renovations, there's the day that is my husband's favorite—demo day. Out with the ugly wallpaper, the pastel pink tile, the pea green formica; in with the swinging mallet, crowbar, and jackhammer. Just as Matt takes delight in destroying the old so that we can breathe something new, the Lord delights in bursting our bonds (Ps. 107:14). He delights in setting us free! It's not a chore for Him. He's not rolling His eyes saying, "really?"

> *Is this something that is hard for you to believe? If it is, take this opportunity to pray the simple prayer found in Mark 9:24: "I believe; help my unbelief!"*

Although we've come to the end of Week Three, for many of us, it is just the beginning. Learning to live in the light takes time, patience, and mounds of grace. We will stumble forward, falling more times than we'd like, but if we're willing to confess and repent (as 1 John encourages us), He will graciously set us back on our feet. As the old adage says, "two steps forward and one step back is still one step forward."

> *Do you need to "walk in the light" concerning what you've discovered this week? Do you need to confess the hurt, the substance, or relationship you're hooked on, or the sin you just can't shake? James 5:16 encourages us to confess our sins to one another so that we may be healed. Bring it into the light with someone you trust. Let Him do His work. It's worth it.*

FOLLY

Some were fools through their sinful ways,
    and because of their iniquities suffered affliction;
they loathed any kind of food,
    and they drew near to the gates of death.
Then they cried to the LORD in their trouble,
    and he delivered them from their distress.
He sent out his word and healed them,
    and delivered them from their destruction.
Let them thank the LORD for his steadfast love,
    for his wondrous works to the children of man!
And let them offer sacrifices of thanksgiving,
    and tell of his deeds in songs of joy!
PSALM 107:17-22

DISCUSSION QUESTIONS:

What do you think of when you hear the word *folly*?

Do you have a story of folly in your own life?

How do we avoid folly by trusting in our loving Father?

Has there been a place of folly in your life that's been exposed? What was that like?

Day One
WHAT IS FOLLY?

READ PSALM 107—ALOUD, IF POSSIBLE.

With which section of the psalm can you most readily identify this time?

Which section is puzzling this time?

This week we will be focusing on verses 17 through 22. I have affectionately named this section Folly. Let's dig in to see why.

We haven't broken out our dictionaries in quite a while! Did you think I forgot about them? Well, crack them open (or pull up your Web browser) and get ready.

Look up the definition of "folly" and write down what you find.

You probably could have answered the question "what is folly" without looking up the definition, but sometimes various definitions of a word can shine a new light on our understanding of it. The definition I found included words like unwise, foolish, absurd (naturally) but also costly (which I hadn't necessarily considered before).[1]

FOLLY'S ATTRIBUTES

Read what Proverbs has to say about folly:

The woman Folly is loud;
she is seductive and knows nothing.
She sits at the door of her house;
she takes a seat on the highest places of the town,
calling to those who pass by,
who are going straight on their way,
"Whoever is simple, let him turn in here!"
And to him who lacks sense she says,
"Stolen water is sweet,
and bread eaten in secret is pleasant."
But he does not know that the dead are there,
that her guests are in the depths of Sheol.

PROVERBS 9:13-18

Name at least three things you can gather from this description of folly.

One doesn't have to lean in to hear folly. It's usually the first and loudest voice we hear as sinful, fallen human beings. In fact, it sounds a lot like the serpent's voice in the garden:

Did God really say ...?
He is holding out on you!
He can't be trusted!
Take matters into your own hands!
You deserve better.
You are the point; life is about you.

What are some other phrases folly has whispered in your ear or you've heard in your heart?

Seductive and enticing, isn't it? We want to hear that we would make a better god than God. If the Lord would just get with OUR program, then things would be much better. The truth is, folly knows nothing. It is earthly wisdom—wisdom that is driven by what makes sense to us without regard to what God says is right, true, and good. Folly fights for the "now." It cares nothing of consequences. "Eat, drink, and be merry with no concern for tomorrow" is its motto.

TOXIC

The problem with living for now is that you are still sowing something that will bear fruit in your life sooner or later (and it's usually sooner than we'd all like). I found an article in a magazine not long ago that illustrates this point. Roughly forty years ago, a paper company contracted a waste management company to dispose of their industrial waste. They dug deep pits alongside a river and buried the waste. Once the pits were full, the area was abandoned. Slowly, the land between the pits and the river began to erode. Toxins from the industrial waste started seeping into the river. Years later, a hurricane hit the area causing flooding which further distributed the toxins. Residents of the town nearby started falling mysteriously ill—multiple myeloma, lupus, and lymphoma, among others.[2]

The faulty manner in which the waste was disposed showed little care for the future and wreaked havoc on the health of the residents. Folly brought forth affliction. This is true of the people in Psalm 107 and of us when we buy into earthly wisdom. In verse 17 where it says "suffered affliction," it means they afflicted themselves.[3]

Are there areas of your life where you knowingly operate according to earthly wisdom? How has that affected you and others?

What are some "toxins" that bubble up from folly?

Read James 3:13-16 and make a list of the earthly wisdom you find.

I would also add one more: anxiety. When we live according to earthly wisdom, all the onus is on us. We're God, right? We know what's best, right? But we're not and we don't. We've put ourselves on God's throne, making decrees and falling miserably short. We feel our inadequacy and inability to sustain life. We are not God. We are not the point of life. This is not all there is. Life reveals these truths pretty quickly. Folly refuses to accept it.

Are there areas in your life where you place yourself on God's throne? Have you experienced anxiety as a result? Explain.

FOODLIKE SUBSTANCES

In verse 18 of Psalm 107, what does it say they "loathed"?

I would like to posit that since this was before the junk food era, one could infer this meant any kind of "real" food. Michael Pollan, in his book *In Defense of Food*, makes this observation about our modern eating habits:

Because most of what we're consuming today is not food, and how we're consuming it—in the car, in front of the TV, and increasingly alone—is not really eating. Instead of food, we're consuming "edible foodlike substances"—no longer the products of nature but of food science.[4]

I want to borrow Mr. Pollan's term for junk food to describe the spiritual foodlike substances that we consume in the midst of folly. Let's take a look back at the Israelites coming out of Egypt and see how they might have "loathed any kind of [real] food."

Read Numbers 11:4-8 and answer the following: Who had a strong craving? Who was this "rabble"? (See Ex. 12:38.)

What were they and the Israelites complaining about?

What had God provided for them?

What did it cost to eat what God gave them?

What had it cost them to eat what Egypt provided?

The rabble were those who had intermarried with the Egyptians. Don't be misled: This wasn't an ethnicity issue. It was a trust issue. This group of people symbolized Israel's propensity to trust man rather than God. In taking Egyptians as husbands or wives, they were essentially buying into earthly wisdom. They placed themselves back on the throne to reign over and rule their own lives, to be the point and to only consider the here and now. What they couldn't see from the vantage point of their wedding day in Egypt was the refining heat of the wilderness—when their faith would be tested. The trust they had put in Egypt, in man, would rear its head as a rabble, a loud minority stirring up trouble and revealing Israel's folly.

The Israelites had a false perception of reality. God provided exactly what they needed for free. No labor was demanded to reap it. The manna appeared in the morning and the quail came on its own. There was no toil in it for them, nor an exchange of goods. Egypt's bounty? The cucumbers, melons, leeks, onions and garlic? Their price tag? Harsh servitude, enslavement—their very lives.

Remember when Jesus was tempted by Satan in the wilderness? The enemy prodded Him to turn a rock into bread. But Jesus responded: "It is written, "'Man shall not live by bread alone, but by every word that comes from the mouth of God'" (Matt. 4:4). God's Word is the real food. But when we're stuck in a season of folly, we have no appetite for it. Our palates are accustomed to the empty calories of earthly wisdom. We feed on nothing, wasting away bit by bit and bite by bite. We "[draw] near to the gates of death" (Ps. 107:18).

How about you? Are you subsisting on spiritual foodlike substances and loathing "real food"? Make a list of the foodlike substances—the "proverbs" of earthly wisdom—by which you live.

Close today by looking at your list. Are you embarrassed? Ashamed? Don't be. We all are tempted to feed on our own wisdom. As I mentioned before, one of the sayings at our church goes, "It's okay to not be okay; you just can't stay there."

Make the following excerpt of a psalm your prayer:

- -

How can a young man keep his way pure?
By guarding it according to your word.
With my whole heart I seek you;
let me not wander from your commandments!
I have stored up your word in my heart,
that I might not sin against you.
Blessed are you, O Lord;
teach me your statutes!
With my lips I declare
all the rules of your mouth.
In the way of your testimonies I delight
as much as in all riches.
I will meditate on your precepts
and fix my eyes on your ways.
I will delight in your statutes;
I will not forget your word.

PSALM 119:9-16

- -

Day Two
FEAR OF THE LORD

Before we move on to the main focus of today's study, I want to pay attention to the second half of the verse where we left off yesterday. Turn to Psalm 107. (Your Bible should fall naturally to this place now that we've camped out here so long!) Note especially verse 18. We've already covered the first half of the verse—"they loathed any kind of food."

What does the last half say?

If you are "drawing near" to something, are you an active agent or passive agent? In other words, is this an action you are doing or is being done to you? Explain.

Write down what Proverbs 14:12 and Proverbs 16:25 say.

I'll be honest, I didn't know this verse was written in Proverbs twice. The Lord must have a good reason for this. He doesn't repeat Himself because He forgot He said it the first time. We would be wise to perk up our ears.

How do these verses connect to Psalm 107:18?

GATES

To continue in our pursuit of earthly wisdom is the quickest way to the gates of death. We're always drawing near to something, some kind of gate. The lame man in Acts 3 who "drew near" to the temple gate called Beautiful comes to mind.

The story goes that a man "lame from birth" was carried by some benevolent men every day to sit at the temple gate and beg for alms (money or food given to the poor). Every single day, he put himself at the mercy of people walking into the temple to worship.

One day, his drawing near to that gate produced more than he could have imagined. I'm sure a good day in his eyes was receiving enough alms to fall asleep that night with a full stomach. The Lord had a better idea. The man called out to Peter and John (two of Jesus' disciples) as they passed by. Upon seeing him, Peter told the man to look up at them. Side note: have you ever encountered someone begging for money or food? How often do you or they make eye contact? In my experience, it happens rarely. To look someone in the eye is to acknowledge their dignity as a human being. I love that Peter did that.

The next words out of Peter's mouth probably dashed the man's hopes: "I have no silver and gold …" But he didn't stop. "What I do have I give to you. In the name of Jesus Christ of Nazareth, rise up and walk!" (v. 6). Then Peter grabbed him by his right hand and raised him up. His feet and ankles immediately became strong and he leapt in praise of what God had done.

I can only speculate why that man was willing to be carried every day to the Beautiful Gate. My best guess is that there was not much else he could do. He couldn't work. He couldn't earn a living. His only other option was to waste away at home (whatever that may have looked like). Drawing near to the gate called Beautiful meant some kind of life. Little did he know how miraculous that life would turn out to be.

In our earthly wisdom, we unknowingly draw near to the gates of death. But there's a better way. It's a way that leads to life, if we would draw near.

TRUE WISDOM

If earthly wisdom is folly, what is true wisdom? How do we get it? It would make sense to find the answer in one of the books included in the "wisdom literature" of Scripture—Proverbs.

Complete the following from Proverbs 9:10.

The _____ of the _____ is the _____ of _____, and the _____ of the _____ _____ is _____.

So our answer? "The fear of the LORD is the beginning of wisdom." I can feel you staring blankly at this. It's okay. What on earth is the fear of the Lord? I thought we aren't supposed to be afraid of God. Remember, perfect love casts out fear. The Lord tells Joshua a bunch of times, "do not fear." Could this be right?

Let me assure you, it's right. In most occurrences of "do not fear" in Scripture, we could place "man" at the end of it. Don't be afraid of what man can do to you— how he could make you suffer, embarrass, shame, or reject you, or what he could take from you.

What does Jesus say about fear in Matthew 10:28?

What does He go on to say about "him who can destroy both soul and body in hell" (vv. 29-31)?

HOLY FEAR

There is a holy fear that is appropriate and necessary when approaching the Lord. He is powerful and terribly magnificent. He could extinguish us as a candle's flame. But He's also gracious, merciful, slow to anger, and abounding in steadfast love. The prophet Isaiah had an encounter with the Lord that illustrates God's terrifying magnificence and profound mercy.

Read Isaiah 6:1-8 and answer the following questions:
What significant event marked the year Isaiah is referencing?

According to 2 Chronicles 26:16-21, what happened to King Uzziah and why?

Besides being an actual king, what could King Uzziah possibly represent here?

Back to Isaiah 6:1-8. Who does Isaiah see? What word do the angels repeat three times?

How does Isaiah respond to what he sees and hears?

What happens after Isaiah's response?

Now, with your finger or bookmark saving your place in Isaiah, flip over to Exodus 20:18-21. Answer the following:
What did the people see and hear? How did they respond?

What does Moses say to the people? Notice anything odd about it?

John Piper interprets Moses' exhortation to the people:

The fear that Moses was telling them to get rid of was the fear of coming close to God and hearing his voice. The fear that Moses wanted them to keep before their eyes was that God is fearfully powerful and opposed to sin. The fear of kindling God's powerful wrath against sin ought not to drive us away from God but to God for mercy.[5]

Let's compare and contrast these two encounters:

ISAIAH'S ENCOUNTER
AND RESPONSE

ISRAEL'S ENCOUNTER
AND RESPONSE

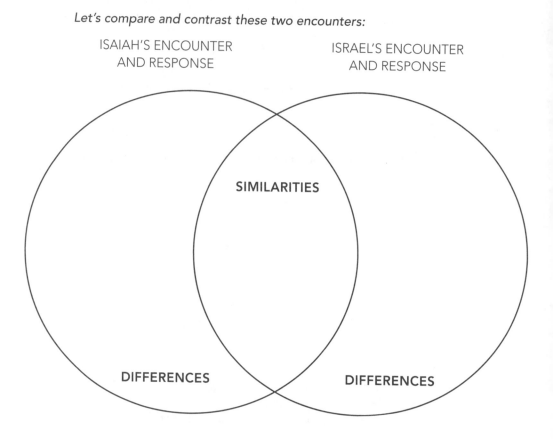

SIMILARITIES

DIFFERENCES

DIFFERENCES

Let's tie this back to the beginning of today's homework. Imagine Isaiah's encounter and response is one "gate" and Israel's encounter and response is another. When Isaiah was met with the formidable holiness of God, he responds in fear but a fear differentiated by Moses' speech to the Israelites—a fear of God's wrath against sin. He knows his guilt and the guilt of his people. He knows that they have sought earthly wisdom and feared man more than God. They are not worthy to stand in the Lord's presence nor speak a word. Instead of keeping his distance, he draws near to the Lord and the Lord draws near to him. Isaiah knows that his only chance is the mercy of the one who is able to "destroy both soul and body in hell." What is he met with? A burning coal on his lips and absolution—God's purifying mercy.

We are drawing near to one of the two gates: the gate of holy fear of God (true wisdom) which leads to life and the gate of the fear of man (earthly wisdom) which leads to death. Like the lame man, drawing near to the gate that leads to life might not look like what we thought it would. It might be hard to swallow.

We might not hear what we want to hear ("I have no silver and gold"), but we will receive life ("In the name of Jesus Christ of Nazareth, rise up and walk!").

If we continue to buy into earthly wisdom, believing we can make a better god, believing our truth supersedes the truth of God, it means affliction and eventually death. So how do we draw near to the gate that leads to life?

Read Psalm 107:19 and write it below.

Those in folly did just what those in the desert and in chains did. They cried out to the Lord. They humbled themselves, recognizing that their earthly wisdom wasn't working. Their wisdom had dried up—they knew that they didn't know. But they knew they could know the One who does. No longer looking inward and downward, they looked outward and upward to Him.

Take this moment to cry out to the Lord. Confess any fear of man or earthly wisdom that keeps you drawing near to the gates of death. Receive the mercy that is available to you through Christ. Ask the Lord to help you to walk in repentance—fearing Him and trusting He makes a much better God.

Day Three
GOD'S INCOMMUNICABLE TRAITS

Thanks to all the hard work we put in yesterday, we know that the way out of folly is to rightly fear the Lord. To do so, we must rightly see Him. This goes back to calling on Him as "the LORD."

Do you remember what "the LORD," or Yahweh, means?

Write 1 Timothy 6:16 below.

Circle the titles and descriptors (we'll call them attributes for the following exercise) from the passage above that only can be said about God. Write them in the first column. Then, write the definition of each in the second column (feel free to use a dictionary, other resource, or write it in your own words).

ATTRIBUTE	DEFINITION

COMMUNICABLE VS. INCOMMUNICABLE

These traits are called His "incommunicable attributes."

Does the word "incommunicable" sound familiar? What would be your best guess at its definition?

When I hear the word *incommunicable*, I think of its opposite: communicable. Being a mother of three, I know the word usually precedes "diseases." During the infant and toddler years, I was always very aware of communicable diseases like RSV, the flu, strep throat, and the oft dreaded Norovirus (in layman's terms, the big, bad stomach bug). If there was even a whiff of someone's aunt's good friend's hair stylist with the stomach bug, that person was knocked off the playdate list for at least a few weeks (I kid!—kind of).

The incommunicable traits of God are the attributes of Him that cannot be "caught" or passed on to others. These include His independence, immutability, omnipresence, eternal nature, omnipotence, sovereignty, omniscience, wisdom, holiness, wrath, and love.

If you're like me, you saw some of those traits and thought, *Wrath and love? I've got plenty of both!* Just wait. Trust me.

Following you'll find a chart with four columns. I have filled out some of the boxes, but lucky you get to finish them! The first column has been completely filled (you're welcome). For the second column you may use a dictionary or your own words if you already know the definition. In the third column list the implication that attribute has on creation. Lastly, the fourth column is for the evidence among humans that we do not share this attribute with God. Note: As with most studies of God's character and attributes, our finite human minds are only able to grasp a limited perspective of all that He is. Notable theological scholars vary in opinion as to which qualities of God are incommunicable and communicable. We'll prayerfully use these labels for the purposes of our study together as handholds to grasp a deeper understanding of who He is.

ATTRIBUTE WITH SCRIPTURE REFERENCE	DEFINITION	IMPLICATION	THE HUMAN DIFFERENCE
ETERNAL NATURE (Ps. 90:2; cf. Ex. 3:14; Job 36:26; Ps. 90:4; Isa. 46:9-10; John 8:58; 1 Tim. 6:16; 2 Pet. 3:8; Jude 24-25; Rev. 1:8; 4:8)	God doesn't have a beginning or an end. He was not made. He is not limited by time and space.	Our hearts can take comfort, despite our human frailty and mortality, in the safety of a God who is not bound by time.	We have a beginning. We haven't always been. Right now, we are bound by time and space. We are limited to the here and now.
HOLINESS (Rev. 4:8; Ex. 15:11; 1 Chron. 16:27-29; Isa. 57:15 Isa. 5:16; 6:1-8; Acts 3:14; Heb. 7:26)			
IMMUTABILITY (Mal. 3:6; Ps. 102:25-27; Jas. 1:17; Ps. 33:11; Isa. 46:9-11; Num. 23:19; Rom. 11:29)			
INDEPENDENCE (Acts 17:24-25; Ex. 3:14; Job 41:11; Ps. 50:9-12; 90:2)			
LOVE (1 John 4:8-10; John 3:16; 15:13; 17:24; Rom. 5:8; 8:31-39; Gal. 2:20; 1 John 3:16; 4:16)			
OMNIPOTENCE (Isa. 46:9-10; Ex. 6:3; Job 37:23; 40:2; 42:1-6; Ps. 24:6; 33:10-11; 91:1; Dan. 4:34-35; Matt. 28:18)			

ATTRIBUTE WITH SCRIPTURE REFERENCE	DEFINITION	IMPLICATION	THE HUMAN DIFFERENCE
OMNIPRESENCE (Jer. 23:23-24; 1 Kings 8:27; Ps. 139:7-10; Isa. 66:1-2; Acts 7:48-50)			
OMNISCIENCE (1 John 3:20; Job 28:24; 37:16; Ps. 139:1-3; 147:5; Isa. 55:8-9; Matt. 10:29-30; Rom. 11:33-34; 1 Cor. 2:10-11; Heb. 4:13)			
SOVEREIGNTY (Dan. 4:34-35; 1 Chron. 29:11-13; Ps. 22:28; 24:1; 47:7-9; 103:19; Prov. 16:19,21,33; Dan. 4:25; 7:1-28; 12:1-13; Matt. 6:13; 10:29; Acts 17:26; Eph. 1:11; 1 Tim. 6:15; Jas. 1:13-15)			
WISDOM (Dan. 2:20; Job 9:4; 12:13; Ps. 104:24; Rom. 11:33; 16:27; 1 Cor. 1:21-29; Eph. 3:10-11)			
WRATH (Rev. 6:15-16; cf. Ex. 34:7; Rom. 1:18; 2:4; 2 Cor. 5:10; 2 Thess. 1:5; 2 Pet. 3:9)			

Adapted from The ESV Study Bible. [6]

Okay, that was a lot of work. Great job getting through it! The two attributes that seem to be communicable are love and wrath. Hopefully you discovered the difference between God *being* love and having wrath toward sin versus our fickle love and selective wrath.

Which attribute surprised you the most?

Which implication means the most to you? Why?

Which attribute do you tend to think of as a communicable one?

Take a moment, as we close, to thank God for each attribute that is not like us. Thank Him for how you specifically experience it in your life. Thank Him for the ones that are hard for you to believe but Scripture says are true.

PURIFIED

Then they cried to the LORD in their trouble,
and he delivered them from their distress.

PSALM 107:19

Put yourself back in Isaiah's shoes in Isaiah 6. Take time to visualize the scene as best you can. Close your eyes if you need to. Smell the smoke. Feel the trembling thresholds. Let your ears ring with the booming echo of the seraphim's cry, "Holy, holy, holy is the LORD of hosts; the whole earth is full of his glory!"

What was remarkable about the seraphim's physical appearance?

Why do you think they had wings covering their faces and feet?

ISAIAH'S RESPONSE

What were Isaiah's first words?

In the magnificent presence of God, even the angels must cover the glory of their faces and the lesser honor of their feet. If they have to cover up, how much more would sinful man?

Have you ever been in a place where someone walked in and you immediately felt underdressed? What was your first inclination?

When we rightly see God and rightly fear Him, we start to see where we don't measure up. We begin to acknowledge that our earthly wisdom is folly. How could we know what God knows? We are but a measly breath!

I am reminded of Job's humble response to the Lord's challenge of him in Job 42:1-6.

> Then Job answered the LORD and said:
> "I know that you can do all things,
> and that no purpose of yours can be thwarted.
> 'Who is this that hides counsel without knowledge?'
> Therefore I have uttered what I did not understand,
> things too wonderful for me, which I did not know.
> 'Hear, and I will speak;
> I will question you, and you make it known to me.'
> I had heard of you by the hearing of the ear,
> but now my eye sees you;
> therefore I despise myself,
> and repent in dust and ashes."

Job's and Isaiah's responses are the same—they knew they were in trouble apart from God's mercy.

GOD'S RESPONSE

How did God respond to Isaiah?

The burning coal was purification by fire, not punishment. From this passage, the theologian Matthew Henry concludes that "God has strong consolations ready for holy mourners."[7] He also notes that the seraphim flew to Isaiah immediately upon his confession. God didn't wait to purify; He instigated it promptly.

Take heart, friend. If, in studying God's attributes yesterday and picturing in your mind's eye God's magnificent presence before Isaiah today, you have felt overwhelmed with guilt and inadequacy, you are exactly where you need to be. Remember, though, in that guilt and inadequacy, not to run away from the Lord but run to Him. He is eager and ready to receive you and your confession and "cleanse [you] from all unrighteousness" (1 John 1:9).

Now, some of you may be thinking, why did it take a burning coal to purify Isaiah? Why not use a bar of soap like my grandma used when our parents (as kids) said an inappropriate word?

What do you think? Why do you think it took fire and not soap?

The degree of purification is indicative of the degree of the impurity. God's wrath burns white-hot against sin because of sin's affront to a holy God. God hates sin and His hate is directly proportional to His love. If He loved little, He would hate little. But because He loves us intensely, His wrath is equally intense. We see this perfectly in Jesus' crucifixion.

Earthly wisdom would have had Jesus coming to teach us how to be good enough. Jesus would have been our life coach equipping us with the tools to do life right. Essentially, He would have said, "you've got this! You just need a little extra help!" But that's not what happened. Jesus came to die. And it was an ugly, dishonorable death.

Read John 19 (aloud, if possible). Now, read Isaiah 53.

Isaiah 53 was written hundreds of years before the events of John 19. What parallels do you see? In what ways did Jesus fulfill this prophecy?

The searing wrath of God was poured out on Jesus so that those who would trust in His salvation alone by faith alone would receive grace and mercy. This is why we call it the gospel—the good news.

But he was pierced for our transgressions;
he was crushed for our iniquities;
upon him was the chastisement that brought us peace,
and with his wounds we are healed.
All we like sheep have gone astray;
we have turned—every one—to his own way;
and the LORD has laid on him
the iniquity of us all.

ISAIAH 53:5-6

Seems like an unfair trade, doesn't it? Jesus lived a perfectly obedient life, never broke a rule or commandment on the outside or the inside. He always submitted to the will of the Father. He was wisdom incarnate. And He willingly gave up His life for us. We get eternal life when we deserve death and separation from God. We get mercy when we deserve justice. This sounds like folly, but it is the beginning of wisdom.

What does 1 Corinthians 1:18 say?

What appears as folly to earthly wisdom is, in reality, true wisdom.

But God chose what is foolish in the world to shame the wise;
God chose what is weak in the world to shame the strong;
God chose what is low and despised in the world, even things
that are not, to bring to nothing things that are, so that no
human being might boast in the presence of God.

1 CORINTHIANS 1:27-29

We get to be weak and foolish in the eyes of the world—according to earthly wisdom. We get to cry out to God in His holiness and majesty and be met with mercy and grace that purifies us. He delivers us from the fruit of our folly—destruction and, eventually, death.

Day Five
HEALED

- -

He sent out his word and healed them,
and delivered them from their destruction.

PSALM 107:20

- -

Words are powerful. Proverbs 18:21 tells us that "death and life are in the power of the tongue." Although it is small in size, it can boast great things. In James 3 it is likened to a spark that is able to set a forest aflame.

I would guess at some point in your life someone has spoken a word that has either built you up or torn you down in a way that you still remember. Is this true of you? If so, how does it affect you today?

If words uttered by humans have so much power, how much more do the words of God? Consider the creation story in Genesis 1. What did God do to make the heavens and earth? Choose the best answer:
☐ Formed them with His hands
☐ Gave instructions to the angels to build them
☐ Spoke them into existence
☐ Took ingredients out of the cosmos and baked them like a cake

God's words have the power to create life. There are times I would love to have that much power. This usually happens when I'm lying in bed, about to start my day, and wishing I could speak a cup of hot coffee into existence onto my nightstand. Alas, the Lord knows what He's doing in not giving me that kind of power with my words.

In Psalm 107:20, once the people in folly cry out to the Lord for deliverance, what does it say He did?

REAL FOOD

Look back over the rest of the psalm, specifically verses 7, 14, and 20. The Lord responds to those in distress according to their need. For those in the desert, He leads them to a city. For those in chains, He bursts their bonds apart. For those suffering the consequences of their folly, He sends out His word and heals them.

The Lord knows exactly what we need in order to deliver us from our distress. For those in folly, we need the healing power of His Word.

On Day One of this week, what did we find the people in folly were feeding on?

What did they loathe?

So, what is real food? Turn to Deuteronomy 8:1-3. Read the passage and answer the following questions:

What is meant by "whole commandment" (your version may say "every command" or "all the commandments") we are to carefully follow in verse 1?

What does it say the Lord used the forty years in the wilderness to do?

Why did God give the people manna?

Read Matthew 4:1-4 and note the similarities with the passage in Deuteronomy 8.

Our work today has led us back to a passage we discussed in Week Two—The Desert. This is the beauty of Scripture—there are layers upon layers of diamonds to be mined. We may think we've marveled at all there is in one passage only to discover it again in a whole new way. Jesus was led by the Spirit into the wilderness just as the Israelites were led into the wilderness by the Lord. For forty days and forty nights, Jesus went hungry. For forty years, the Lord let His people hunger so that He might humble and test them to know what was in their hearts, to see if they would keep His commandments. Where they failed, Jesus triumphed. When tempted to turn stones into loaves of bread, He responded with the truth—"man does not live by bread alone, but ... by every word that comes from the mouth of the Lord" (Deut. 8:3).

The real food—true sustenance—is the Word of God. The Lord speaks life through all of Scripture.

All Scripture is breathed out by God and profitable for teaching, for reproof, for correction, and for training in righteousness, that the man of God may be complete, equipped for every good work.

2 TIMOTHY 3:16-17

Becoming wise means not only fearing the Lord, but knowing His Word. Whether we realize it or not, our souls long for the Word of God. Let's borrow the food illustration again. When we crave junk food, it's usually because it is fast, easy, and accessible; but our bodies truly need the nutrients found in real food. The same is true spiritually.

What does Psalm 119:20 say?

There's a warning we should heed, though. In John 5, Jesus heals a man who has been lame for thirty-eight years. That wouldn't seem like a problem, right? To the Pharisees (the most religious Jews), it was an abomination. Jesus healed the man on the Sabbath. In their eyes, He had broken the Sabbath. The act of healing was not on their list of acceptable practices on what was meant to be a day of rest. They took what God said and twisted it to suit their preferences. The Pharisees missed the whole point. Jesus calls them on it saying, "You search the Scriptures because you think that in them you have eternal life; and it is they that bear witness about me, yet you refuse to come to me that you may have life" (vv. 39-40).

We need the nutrients of God's words and we need to know the Word of God. John 1:1 speaks of the Word of God (Jesus). What does it say about Him?

Our healing is only found in Jesus—the Word made flesh. He is the life that is the light of men. We devour Scripture so that we may know God, that we may see Him and love Him. It's folly to know His Word without knowing Him.

Do you know His Word but don't know Him? Or are you attempting to "know God" without knowing His Word?

WISDOM FROM ABOVE

As folly bears its fruit, wisdom has its own. Do you remember the fruit (or "toxins") of folly from Day One in James 3? Write them here:

Read James 3:17-18 and record wisdom's fruit:

Take each of these fruits, define them, and then measure your life against them.

PURE
   Definition:

   In your life:

PEACEABLE
   Definition:

   In your life:

GENTLE
   Definition:

   In your life:

OPEN TO REASON
   Definition:

   In your life:

FULL OF MERCY
   Definition:

   In your life:

FULL OF GOOD FRUITS
Definition:

In your life:

IMPARTIAL
Definition:

In your life:

SINCERE
Definition:

In your life:

Repenting of folly and turning to wisdom from above brings peace with God and peace with others. It also delivers us from destruction. In the last half of Psalm 107:20, those in folly are delivered from their destruction. The word translated as *destruction* literally means "grave pits."[8]

The more we try to dig ourselves out of the consequences of folly, the deeper we bury ourselves in the grave. While studying Psalm 107, I noticed somewhat of a domino effect from the desert to chains to folly. The broken cisterns of which we refuse to repent become prisons. The prisons and the chains that bind us of which we refuse to cry out to the Lord for rescue become grave pits.

Have you seen this effect in your life? How so?

To close, make Psalm 40 your prayer today. Read the psalm out loud. Own it. Make it your sacrifice of thanksgiving and song of joy (Ps. 107:22).

Week Five

STORM

Some went down to the sea in ships,
doing business on the great waters;
they saw the deeds of the LORD,
his wondrous works in the deep.
For he commanded and raised the stormy wind,
which lifted up the waves of the sea.
They mounted up to heaven; they went down to the depths;
their courage melted away in their evil plight;
they reeled and staggered like drunken men
and were at their wits' end.
Then they cried to the LORD in their trouble,
and he delivered them from their distress.
He made the storm be still,
and the waves of the sea were hushed.
Then they were glad that the waters were quiet,
and he brought them to their desired haven.
Let them thank the LORD for his steadfast love,
for his wondrous works to the children of man!
Let them extol him in the congregation of the people,
and praise him in the assembly of the elders.

PSALM 107:23-32

DISCUSSION QUESTIONS:

How have storms in your life affected the way you see God? The way you see yourself?

How do we know what our anchors currently are? How do we make God our anchor before the storm hits?

How have you seen God provide the grace necessary for the storms in your life?

How can we find God's presence in our everyday lives and in the storms?

Day One
AT SEA

READ PSALM 107—ALOUD, IF POSSIBLE.

With which section of the psalm can you most readily identify this time?

Which section is puzzling this time?

Look at verses 23-32. What is this group of people doing? In what kind of business would you guess they were involved?

What did they see?

OCCUPATIONAL HAZARDS

The people in this section of the psalm are simply going about their business. They are going to work, likely dealing in trade or fishing. Sure, they know storms are an occupational hazard, but storms always seem to strike suddenly.

Have you ever been in the middle of a storm on the ocean? If so, what was it like?

The only time I have experienced a storm at sea was on our honeymoon. In fact, it rained almost every day of our honeymoon cruise. If omens were a thing, I'd think we were in for some trouble! I recall one evening at dinner the waves were significantly tossing our ship about. I noticed the liquid in all of our glasses was at a 45° angle. Although most in the dining room couldn't finish their dinner, we were all fairly safe.

The ocean liners of today are nothing like the merchant ships in the ancient world. In fact, *The Black Pearl*, Jack Sparrow's ship from *Pirates of the Caribbean*, would have been an upgrade for them. While a cruise ship could weather a significant storm with only seasick passengers, the passengers on ancient ships would be at risk for their lives. When it comes to the storms of life, we are much less like the modern cruise ships and more like the merchant ships. In the sage words of the musician Sting, "how fragile we are."[1] Storms are an occupational hazard of life. It's not a matter of *if* but *when*.

Write Proverbs 16:9 in your own words.

In 2009, our family planned to take our first trip together to Disney World over Christmas break. Our plane tickets were booked, hotel reservations made, and dreams of our children's delight when seeing Mickey and Minnie danced in our heads. However, it wasn't meant to be. On Thanksgiving Day, our plans came crashing down. Matt suffered a grand mal seizure that revealed a malignant brain tumor. A week later he was under the knife. For the next eighteen months, he endured radiation and chemotherapy. No Disney, but we did feel like we were in a whole new world. We made plans but the Lord established our steps.

Has a storm overtaken you like that? Are you in the middle of one right now? Briefly describe your storm.

PARADISE LOST

You may be asking yourself, why would the Lord establish such painful steps? What's wrong with a family vacation? First, storms and the suffering they bring are a part of the fall (Gen. 3).

Revisit our ancestors, Adam and Eve, in Genesis 1 and 3. Complete the following:

Genesis 1:26—

Then God said, "Let us make man in our image, after our likeness. And let them have _____ over the _____ of the _____ and over the _____ of the _____ and over the _____ and over all the _____ and over every _____ that creeps on the earth."

Genesis 1:28—

And God blessed them. And God said to them, "Be _____ and _____ and _____ the earth and _____ it, and have _____ over the fish of the sea and over the birds of the heavens and over every living thing that moves on the earth."

Genesis 3:8—

And they _____ the sound of the _____ _____ walking in the _____ in the cool of the day, and the man and his wife hid themselves from the presence of the LORD *God among the trees of the garden.*

Here's what Adam and Eve enjoyed before the fall: unhindered dwelling, dominion, and dynasty. God made His dwelling with them. He walked in the garden in the cool of the day. He gave them dominion over all creation and He tasked them with establishing a dynasty—being fruitful and multiplying and filling the earth with His image bearers.

Can you envision walking with God—in the garden of Eden—in perfection? I have longed for the tangible presence of God, especially in times of great heartache, and I can only imagine what this was like. And the dominion and dynasty part made easy? Yes, please! Something happens, though, as we studied in Week One, in Genesis 3.

Refer to Genesis 3:14-22. How are dwelling, dominion, and dynasty hindered?

Is there hope for Adam and Eve and their descendants? If so, what is the hope?

With Genesis 3:14-22 fresh on your mind, read Romans 8:18-25 and answer these questions:
Who subjected the creation to futility?

In what way did He subject it?

What is creation's groaning likened to?

What parallels do you see here with Genesis 3:14-22?

Although the pain of childbirth can be frightening, for the most part we know that something good will come of it in the end—a precious child. In the same way, creation groans, suffering befalls us, but not without hope. There is a happy ending for those in Christ whether we see it on earth or not. But let's not get ahead of ourselves. I don't want to glide over the pain and the disorienting nature of the storm.

We weren't meant for the storm. We were meant for dwelling, dominion, and dynasty without the curse of separation, toil, and pain. The reality is we will not escape this life without enduring storms. Take heart, friend, there is hope.

Take a moment to pour your heart out to God. Maybe you're in the midst of a storm, or maybe you're frightened of what may come. Confess the pain or fear and ask the Lord to meet you right where you are.

Day Two
LORD OVER THE STORM

For he commanded and raised the stormy wind,
which lifted up the waves of the sea.

PSALM 107:25

Start off, today especially, asking the Lord to give you eyes to see and ears to hear what He wants to show you. Studying the storm seasons can cause us to be paralyzed by fear of the unknown, but we can remember the promise Jesus speaks in John 16:

I have said these things to you, that in me you may have peace. In the world you will have tribulation. But take heart; I have overcome the world.

JOHN 16:33

We can be encouraged that peace will be found in Him who has overcome the world, who is Lord over the storm.

Turn to Mark 4. In verse 1, where is Jesus teaching?

What parable does He teach?

When He was done speaking to the crowd gathered near the sea and it says He was "alone," who asked Him about the meaning of the parable (v. 10)?

In your own words, what did Jesus say each of the following represented?

Seed on the path:

Seed on the rocky ground:

Seed among thorns:

Seed on the good soil:

What does verse 22 say?

In the second parable (vv. 26-29), what does the man do while the seed sprouts and grows? Does he take part in the harvest?

In the last picture of the kingdom (vv. 30-34), what does Jesus liken it to? What do you think He meant by it?

There's debate over whether these parables happened in real time, back to back, or if they were pieced together by Mark (the Gospel writer). Either way, they were placed in sequential order by the inspiration of the Holy Spirit into the canon of Scripture. It seems there is an idea building from the seed sown in different types of soil, to the seed that sprouts and grows on its own without man's help but is harvested by man, to the tiny mustard seed that grows into a plant with large branches. And then there's the seemingly random commentary on a lamp and a basket.

What happens immediately after Jesus teaches the parables?

What if Jesus was preparing His disciples for what was next? What if He was saying, the storm will reveal (bring to light) the seed of God's Word that's in you—whether it has found stony ground, rocky soil, thorns, or good, receptive soil. And when the storm reveals the truth, you can be comforted that I will cause that seed to grow and spread and many will come to know Me through it. You will get to see and participate in the harvest although you had little to do with its growth.

In Mark 4, whose idea was it to go to the other side? What is the exact phrase He uses?

Can you think of another time the Lord has said "let us"?

The phrase "let us" is repeated countless times in the Old and New Testaments. Most often it precedes an act of the will—man's will or God's will—depending on who is saying it. The first time we see the phrase in Scripture is when God decides to create man. He says, "Let us make man in our image, after our likeness" (Gen. 1:26). The next time the phrase is uttered in Scripture, it's the builders of the Tower of Babel who use it. Dissatisfied with making much of their Creator, they exert their desire and will to "make a name for [them]selves" (Gen. 11:4). Let Us make man in Our image—God's will. Let us make a name for ourselves—man's will. Also note the fact that God accomplished His "let us" while the Babel builders never had the chance to finish their task. So when Jesus says, "Let us go across to the other side," we can count on two things: it's the will of God, and it will be accomplished (Mark 4:35).

It's interesting that Jesus talked about a man sleeping and rising night and day in verses 26-29. What was He doing while a tempest struck?

Sidenote: this is another beautiful display of Jesus' fully God and fully man-ness. If you've ever taught, you know it is an exhausting endeavor. He had, no doubt, just spent Himself physically and emotionally preaching to the crowds and then pulling His disciples aside to further their understanding. Jesus was plain tuckered out! But just because He was tired doesn't mean He wasn't still God.

What do the disciples ask Him when they wake Him?

Have you ever found yourself asking God in the middle of your storm, Lord, do You even care? Describe the circumstances.

Who did Jesus rebuke? Is the answer surprising to you? Why?

How does Jesus respond to His disciples?

The disciples likely deserved the same rebuke the wind and waves got but instead of a "peace; be still," He asked them two questions: "Why are you so afraid?" And "have you still no faith?"

Do you think Jesus knew the answers to these questions? If so, why do you think He asked them?

What does verse 41 say the disciples were feeling? What had they been afraid of just moments before?

What question does Jesus ask the disciples in Luke's version of the story? (See Luke 8:25.)

Their fear and faith are closely tied. What they feared revealed where they put their faith. When the wind and waves threatened to capsize their boat, they feared for their lives. When Jesus rebuked the wind and calmed the sea, they feared Him.

Where is your faith? Are you more fearful of the "wind and waves" or the power of God?

I don't want to minimize the wind and waves of your storm. They are real. They cause pain. They're frightening.

If you're in a storm right now, what do the wind and waves look like for you?

The wind and waves are the things we can taste, touch, hear, smell, and see. As much as we'd like to ignore them, they demand attention. C.S. Lewis once wrote:

> We can ignore even pleasure. But pain insists upon being attended to. God whispers to us in our pleasures, speaks in our conscience, but shouts in our pain: it is His megaphone to rouse a deaf world.[2]

The storm is God's severe mercy to show us where our hope is placed. He uses it to bring to light the condition of our hearts—what kind of soil are we? Have we received His Word gladly? Has our affection for Him been short-lived? Did the enemy snatch it away? Have desires for what God can give us choked out the desire to simply have Him?

What about you? What has the storm revealed about your heart?

Let's close here: Remember that it was Jesus' idea to get in the boat and face the storm. Read Mark 5:1. Did they make it to the other side?

Friend, He is able to get you to the other side. It may not look like what you thought it would, but if you would trust Him to be Lord over the storm, He will be your safe haven. But I'm getting ahead of myself. Hold on tight. Help is coming.

Day Three
JONAH

Hopefully you've found your sea legs. We'll continue aboard another boat today. This one is headed for Tarshish.

Open up to Jonah and read all four chapters. (Don't be discouraged; it's about the length of a blog post!)

Why was Jonah on a boat to Tarshish?

Where was he supposed to be going?

What was he supposed to do?

Now, I don't blame Jonah for running. I loathe confrontation and will do just about anything to avoid it. Looks like Jonah felt the same way.

On the map below, Jonah's original location is marked with a star. Circle Nineveh (where God sent Jonah) and then circle Joppa and Tarshish (where Jonah was headed).

I have figuratively "run" from what the Lord has called me to but Jonah's flight brings a whole new dimension. Tarshish (at least the proposed location of the city) is about as far away as one could get from Nineveh. In fact, this was the known world to the people living in Jonah's time. He was literally headed to the other side of the world!

Can you think of a time you ran away from what the Lord had called you to? Elaborate.

Back to the Book of Jonah, in chapter 1 verse 4, who "hurled a great wind upon the sea"? Recognize the name?

What did the sailors do in response to the tempest? What was Jonah doing?

What does the captain say to Jonah?

How do the sailors find out that Jonah is the cause of the storm? What does that reveal about Jonah?

What does Jonah say about himself in verse 9?

Let's pause here for a moment. Here Jonah is, running from the Lord, hiding in the hull of the ship sleeping off his guilty conscience. He has a chance to fess up to the sailors but he waits for the lots to call him out. Finally, he comes to his senses and remembers who he is and whose he is.

The Lord will use the storm to bring us to our senses. He will use the "megaphone" of the storm to rouse us from sleep and awaken us to who we are and whose we are.

Have you experienced this? If so, tell us about it.

What does Jonah tell the men on the ship to do with him? Do they do it?

What does verse 16 say the sailors did?

The sailors took the Jonah approach at first. They tried to carry out their own plan. They didn't want Jonah's blood on their hands, so they rowed hard trying to get back to dry land. When it became clear their task was futile, they finally surrendered. As the waters ceased raging with the offering of Jonah, they realized the Lord truly was the God of heaven, who made the sea and dry land.

What happened to Jonah?

In chapter 2, from where does Jonah offer up his prayer?

How is Jonah delivered from the fish?

What did Jonah do next?

How did the people respond? How did God respond to the people's response?

How did Jonah feel about their response?

What's interesting about his accusation against God?

There's one last curious story at the end of Jonah about a plant and pity. Jonah went out of the city to wait and see how the Lord would ultimately respond to

Nineveh's repentance. The Lord appointed a plant to shade Jonah and keep him from discomfort. Jonah delighted in the shade. But the next morning, the Lord appointed a worm to consume the plant. This angered Jonah, and (again) he despaired of life. Really, Jonah? You've stared death in the face and lived to tell about it!

Does anything sound familiar in Jonah 4:10?

What point do you think the Lord is making?

The abundant grace, mercy, patience, and steadfast love of the Lord toward Jonah is like the shade the plant provides. Jonah did nothing to deserve to be saved from discomfort. He didn't plant the seed or cause it to grow. God did. The Lord is essentially saying, "I will be gracious to whom I will be gracious, and will show mercy on whom I will show mercy" (Ex. 33:19b). If Nineveh would repent, He has the prerogative to be gracious and show them mercy.

Maybe the Lord is showing you His gracious and merciful steadfast love in the midst of this storm. It may be hard for us to see it for the wind and waves. But maybe, just maybe, He is working something deep for our good.

We're not done with the story of Jonah yet. I want us to draw some parallels between his story and ours.

How are we like the sailors?

How are we like Jonah?

Think back to Mark 4. Let's draw parallels between the disciples and Jesus and the sailors and Jonah.
How were the disciples like the sailors?

How was Jesus like Jonah?

How was Jesus unlike Jonah? (See also Luke 11:32.)

Today, as we face our own storms mighty and small, let's look to the One who is greater than Jonah, the One who both sends the wind and calms it for our good and His glory.

Day Four
JESUS, THE BETTER JONAH

Then they cried to the LORD in their trouble,
and he delivered them from their distress.
He made the storm be still,
and the waves of the sea were hushed.

PSALM 107:28-29

We spent a lot of time yesterday getting to know our friend Jonah. He may have been a little whiny and angry, but can't we all identify with him in that? At the end of yesterday's homework, you drew parallels between Jesus and Jonah. I want to lead you further into that work today. I believe it's worthwhile and will deepen our appreciation of Jesus as the better Jonah.

JESUS' MISSION

The mission God gave Jonah was to call out against Nineveh. According to John 3:16-18, what is Jesus' mission?

Unlike Jonah, Jesus didn't shirk His calling. Instead, what does Philippians 2:8 say He did?

Like Jonah, Jesus was found sleeping in the stern while the storm raged. Unlike Jonah, Jesus had the power to deliver them from it. Jesus doesn't just deliver us from the storm at sea but the storm that threatens to obliterate us all—the power of sin and death. As Jonah offered himself as a sacrifice to save the rest of the ship, so Jesus offered Himself as a sacrifice to save those who would trust in Him. He weathered the worst storm for us to show how much He loves us.

JESUS, THE SYMPATHETIC HIGH PRIEST

In weathering the storm of sin and death, Jesus had to face the storms of the human experience. He had to become fully human although He remained fully God.

What storms of the human experience did Jesus face?

☐ *Isaiah 53:7*

☐ *Matthew 8:20*

☐ *John 11:17-35*

What does Hebrews 4:15 say about Him?

Does any of this bring you comfort? If so, in what way?

COVERED

Remember the sailors' words—"O Lord, let us not perish for this man's life, and lay not on us innocent blood, for you, O Lord, have done as it pleased you" (Jonah 1:14). For the Christian, our plea is different. There is no deliverance unless innocent blood is laid on us. We plead the blood of Christ.

Write Hebrews 9:12 here.

Do you know what it means by "the blood of goats and calves"? If so, what does it mean?

The Mosaic law required a blood sacrifice for the atonement of sin. The blood of a goat and a bull was sprinkled on the altar to atone for the sins of the priest and the people. Jesus offered His own blood—pure and innocent—for the sins of the people. He didn't have to make an offering for His sin because He was sinless. And He doesn't have to make it over and over again. Once and for all, His blood speaks a better word—eternal redemption. It cries out, *Covered! Saved!*

The storm of the power of sin and death can only be calmed by admitting that Christ "threw Himself overboard" to atone for our sin. We have no hope for rescue and redemption unless His blood covers us. Comfort is found in knowing our sins are not counted against us, and that the One who leads us into the boat to reach the other side will get us there.

THE SIGN OF JONAH

Look up Luke 11:30 and complete:

For as _____ became a _____ to the _____ of _____,
so will the _____ ____ _____ be to this _____.

What do you think is the sign of Jonah? What does Matthew 12:40 say it is?

What is the "three days and three nights in the heart of the earth"
a reference to?

Jesus' death and resurrection were a sign to the people that the Lord has power over life and death. And as the people of Nineveh were given the chance to repent, so also are those who hear of Jesus' deliverance. Unlike Jonah, Jesus didn't complain about the Father's mercy, He rejoiced in it. Hebrews 12:2 says that it was for the joy set before Him that Christ endured the cross.

How do you picture Jesus' attitude toward you? Do you see Him as Jonah, frustrated at the Father's mercy, or as He really is, rejoicing in the Father's salvation?

Do you see the storm as punishment or mercy? Elaborate.

The storm is scary. It tests our faith and reveals the true condition of our hearts. But I wouldn't trade the seasons in the storm for anything else. As the disciples began to have an inkling of who Jesus was when He calmed the wind and the waves, and just as they were invited to let head knowledge take root in their hearts, so we can come to know Jesus in the midst of the storm.

Write a prayer asking the Lord to show you who Jesus is in the midst of the storm—the one you might be in now or the one that will come later.

Day Five
DESIRED HAVEN

- -

Then they were glad that the waters were quiet,
and he brought them to their desired haven.

PSALM 107:30

- -

When in the midst of our storm, I remember having this feeling
deep inside that I couldn't quite put my finger on. It was an
unsettledness that I struggled to name. I distinctly recall sitting in
a room with women with whom I had studied the Bible for years.
We listened to a woman on the TV open up to Isaiah 33. One phrase
jumped out among the rest.

Write Isaiah 33:5-6 below.

I finally found the word to name the unsettledness: *instability.* "He will be the
stability of your times" was a balm to my soul (Isa. 33:6). What I longed for in the
raging wind and waves was a semblance of stability. My husband was sick: our
future unknown. *Would I be a widowed single mother of three children? Would
my husband's brain survive the toll surgery, chemo, and radiation would have on
it? Would he be unemployable?*

Every prop that, unbeknownst to me, had held me up was knocked out from
under me. The false anchors of health, companionship, and financial stability
were found to be wanting. Only the Lord could be the true anchor—the stability
of my times.

How about you? What false anchors has the storm exposed?

Still he seeks the fellowship of his people and sends them both sorrows and joys in order to detach their love from other things and attach it to himself.[3]

J.I. PACKER

How does that quote hit you? Does it seem narcissistic? Does the Lord sound needy?

What's the truth?

The Lord isn't needy. He is I Am Who I Am. He is enough in and of Himself. He is the only One who is enough for us. And He isn't narcissistic. Narcissism is an "inordinate fascination with ... self."[4] He is the exalted One who dwells on high. He can't think too highly of Himself because there is no one higher.

In fact, it is an act of love for Him to seek fellowship with us by detaching our love from lesser things and attaching it to Him. Only He is enough. Only He is highest. Only He can bear the weight of our need.

Yes, we want the storm to be still. Quiet waters are a welcome sight after the whipping from the wind and waves. But the calm is not enough. We need a safe place to drop anchor—a shelter—a place to catch our breath. He is that place.

SHELTER

Time to break out the dictionaries! What is a haven?

In order for harbors (havens) to be efficient, they must have two important characteristics: depth and protection. The water must be deep enough to allow large ships to drop anchor, and it must be sheltered by prominent land features on several sides from stormy weather. These elements can be found naturally or constructed artificially by dredging and building seawalls and jettys.

Complete the following from Psalm 91:1-2:

He who dwells in the _____ of the _____ _____
will abide in the shadow of the _____.
I will say to the _____, "My _____ and my _____,
my God, in whom I _____."

The Most High provides shelter and protection. He is a refuge and fortress for those who trust in Him. This doesn't mean that all will turn out how we think it should. Remember, since He is Most High, He has the best perspective and the most power. This also doesn't mean we resign ourselves to the fact that He will do whatever He will do. The Lord delights in our asking. Believing in His sovereignty means we know that whatever may come our way, it's what is best for us because He knows the future. The future is a place He already is.

Dr. Timothy Keller marries God's sovereignty, omniscience, and the prayers of the saints in a way our human minds can grasp: "God will only give you what you would have asked for if you knew everything He knows."[5]

Does this bring you comfort? Why or why not?

DEPTH

You might be in the middle of your storm and still reeling from the wind and the waves. And maybe you are struggling to find comfort. Period. As I've said before, we say time and time again at our church, it's okay to not be okay, just don't stay there.

The Lord being our safe harbor, our desired haven, means He is deep enough for our questions. While we should address Him respectfully as God of the universe, for those who have been adopted into His family, we have the right to come to Him as a child approaches her father—not afraid to ask the hard questions, knowing we will be lovingly received.

Are you struggling? What questions do you have for the Lord?

Here's the truth: as Christians, we are never promised an easy life. The Lord is pretty clear that the storms will come.

Write down what Jesus told His disciples in John 16:33 as He neared His betrayal, crucifixion, and death.

He didn't say you might have tribulation or if you have tribulation. He said you will have tribulation. Strongly and clearly He told those whom He loved, *life will be hard, and the storms will come.* But, He says, "take heart." Why? Because He has "overcome the world." He is the Lord over the storm and the Lord with us in the storm.

Read Psalm 23. Take your time and write down phrases or thoughts that stand out to you.

This passage reminds me that although I may walk through the deepest valleys with the darkest shadows, my soul is safe. There is no evil that can overcome me because the Lord is with me. I am comforted by the fact that regardless of what comes my way, whether the loss of my husband, or my children, or reputation, or home, or station in life, it will all be goodness and mercy toward me from the Lord of steadfast love. And one day, I will forever be safe in the house of the Lord.

How do the storms in life prepare us for the life to come?

I want to leave one last prayer from the Psalms with you before we close. I've affectionately titled it, "Anchored."

For the righteous will never be moved;
he will be remembered forever.
He is not afraid of bad news;
his heart is firm, trusting in the LORD.
His heart is steady; he will not be afraid,
until he looks in triumph on his adversaries.

PSALM 112:6-8

Week Six

GRATITUDE

He turns rivers into a desert,
    springs of water into thirsty ground,
a fruitful land into a salty waste,
    because of the evil of its inhabitants.
He turns a desert into pools of water,
    a parched land into springs of water.
And there he lets the hungry dwell,
    and they establish a city to live in;
they sow fields and plant vineyards
    and get a fruitful yield.
By his blessing they multiply greatly,
    and he does not let their livestock diminish.
When they are diminished and brought low
    through oppression, evil, and sorrow,
he pours contempt on princes
    and makes them wander in trackless wastes;
but he raises up the needy out of affliction
    and makes their families like flocks.
The upright see it and are glad,
    and all wickedness shuts its mouth.
Whoever is wise, let him attend to these things;
    let them consider the steadfast love of the LORD.

PSALM 107:33-43

DISCUSSION QUESTIONS:

Tell the group about a physical scar you have. How did you get it? How long have you had it?

If you're willing, share with the group about spiritual scars you may have. How have these circumstances changed your relationship with God?

How do you grow in your gratitude toward God for His grace?

Day One
REMEMBER

This is the last time we'll read through Psalm 107 together. However, I pray it's not the last time you do this by yourself. I also pray that reading through a large chunk of Scripture over and over again has whetted your appetite to do the same on your own.

READ PSALM 107—ALOUD, IF POSSIBLE.

With which section of the psalm can you most readily identify this time?

Which section is puzzling this time?

If you were to give this psalm a title, what would it be?

What's the refrain you notice at the end of each "distress" or "season"?

My favorite holiday to celebrate is Thanksgiving. Gathering as family and loved ones around food and togetherness without the pressure of gift giving and receiving is incredibly appealing to me. As our kids have gotten older, we started a tradition of making a list of ten things for which we're grateful. Each family member reads their list aloud, expresses their gratitude to the Lord in prayer, and then we close by singing the "Doxology."

REMEMBRANCES

One thing required for this activity is the act of remembering. We must call to memory moments or things the Lord has graciously given. We have to think back to thank Him.

Psalm 107 is a recounting of the Lord's faithfulness to those in distress and their living to tell it. The psalmist encourages them to remember all the Lord has done and thank Him for His steadfast love.

The act of remembrance has always been an essential part of worshiping the Lord.

In the Ten Commandments (Ex. 20:1-18), what does God say to remember?

The Lord established feasts and festivals for His people because He knows we humans are prone to forget. Below is a chart of Old Testament feasts and festivals. I've filled in the Scripture references. Complete what's missing.[1]

SCRIPTURE REFERENCE	FEAST/FESTIVAL	SIGNIFICANCE
Exodus 12:2-20; Leviticus 23:5		Commemorates God's deliverance of Israel out of Egypt
Leviticus 23:6-8		Commemorates God's deliverance of Israel out of Egypt. Includes a Day of Firstfruits for the barley harvest
Exodus 23:16; 34:22; Leviticus 23:15-21		Commemorates the giving of the law at Mount Sinai. Includes a Day of Firstfruits for the wheat harvest

SCRIPTURE REFERENCE	FEAST/FESTIVAL	SIGNIFICANCE
Leviticus 23:23-25; Numbers 29:1-6		Day of the blowing of the trumpets to signal the beginning of the civil new year
Leviticus 23:26-33; Exodus 30:10		On this day the high priest makes atonement for the nation's sin. Also a day of fasting
Leviticus 23:33-43; Numbers 29:12-39; Deuteronomy 16:13		Commemorates the forty years of wilderness wandering
Esther 9:26-28		Commemorates the deliverance of the Jewish people in the days of Esther

The commemoration didn't end with the close of the Old Testament. Jesus observed the feasts and festivals during His life on earth. He also instituted another act of remembrance.

Read Luke 22:14-20. What feast was Jesus observing with His disciples?

What new remembrance was Jesus instituting?

What do the elements symbolize?

Clearly, the Lord is serious about us remembering what He has done for us. Why do you think that is?

How have you seen God personally come through for you?

REMINDERS

Remembrances like feasts, festivals, and the Lord's Supper aren't the only means the Lord uses to help us remember. He also gives us reminders. Nothing jogs my memory like a scar or a limp.

Before you read the following passage, let me give you some context. Jacob was the son of Isaac, the grandson of Abraham, who cheated his twin brother out of his birthright and blessing. Understandably, his brother, Esau, sought revenge. Esau threatened to kill Jacob for theft. Jacob sought asylum among his mother's family miles away. Years and wives and children later, he faced an encounter with Esau. He feared for his life. He wasn't sure if time had healed wounds or caused them to fester gangrenous. The night before he was to meet Esau and confront his past, Jacob found himself alone in the dark.

Read Genesis 32:22-32. What was Jacob doing until the "breaking of the day"?

What did the man do to Jacob?

What did Jacob demand from the man? How did the man respond?

What was Jacob's new name? What does it mean?

Who did Jacob believe the man was? How do you know this? Was he right?

Besides a new name and a blessing, what did the Lord leave Jacob with?

What do you think Jacob thought every time his hip ached?

Before Jacob wrestled with God, he presumed upon His grace. The Lord was the God of his father and grandfather. He had yet to become the God of Jacob. Jacob assumed that God's blessing would be on him because it was on the men before him. He was right. God would bless Jacob. And He would make Jacob a blessing to the whole world. The weight of that blessing was not felt by Jacob until he wrestled with the Lord. In His goodness, the Lord left Jacob with a gift—a limp. He afflicted Jacob. He didn't leave him the same. Jacob responded in humility by acknowledging that he shouldn't have been allowed to live. He saw God face-to-face and yet was spared. He saw God's grace and responded with gratitude.

We've gone on quite the journey together. Think back to a distress or hardship in your life that spoke to you. In that situation, did the Lord leave with you some kind of limp? What about a new name and a blessing? Close today by making a list of ten things you are thankful God has done the past five weeks.

1.

2.

3.

4.

5.

6.

7.

8.

9.

10.

Day Two
REJOICING

Have you ever asked yourself, *what is God's will for my life?* Most of the time when I ask this, I'm usually meaning, *what does the Lord want me to do specifically with my life?* This isn't a bad question. It's good to think about our present and our future—if we're making the most of our time and gifts on earth, or if a decision one way or another will bring glory to God. Have you ever wanted to open up your Bible and read: yes, [your name], you should take that job in another state; or, no, [your name], this isn't the house for you? I'll be honest, I have!

Although there isn't that kind of direction for determining the will of God in Scripture, He doesn't leave us completely hanging.

Read 1 Thessalonians 5:16-18 and write it below.

So what is the will of God in Christ Jesus for you?
verse 16:

verse 17:

verse 18:

What does it mean to rejoice? (Break out the dictionary if you need to!)

How is this different from being happy?

Rejoicing isn't only feeling delight but also taking an action toward delight. In the late 1980's, a reggae song took the world by storm. Well, at least in the States—it garnered a Grammy for Song of the Year in 1989. "Don't Worry Be Happy" became a mantra for the times. *Don't worry about it, just be happy!* While a good and pleasant reminder, I believe it oversimplified dealing with our struggles and fighting for joy. Who wouldn't want to just not worry about it and be happy? If only it were that easy!

A commentary on Thessalonians says it this way:

To rejoice always is to see the hand of God in whatever is happening and to remain certain of God's future salvation. Without such conviction joy would not be possible in the face of affliction, suffering, and death.[2]

Look at the following texts and draw out how the above definition of "rejoice always" is true.
Psalm 27:13

Habakkuk 3:17-19

Philippians 4:4-9

What is rejoicing like for you? Does "don't worry be happy" sound like a great plan or does it grate against your nerves? Are you willing to fight for joy—to see the hand of God and remain certain of His future salvation?

Perhaps the most difficult place to rejoice is in the middle of our distress—in the desert, chains, suffering from folly, and the storm.

Read 1 Peter 1:3-9. In verse 6, what is the "this" in which they rejoice?

Also in verse 6, what have the various trials caused them to feel?

What is the "necessary" goal of the trials?

To what is their faith compared? How is it tested?

We don't have to take delight in our circumstances. We can mourn and grieve the wind and waves, the heat and drought, the dark and heavy, and the pain of foolish decisions. What we can take delight in is what God has done through Jesus for us no matter our circumstances. We have been adopted as His children. We have been "born again," and we have a future hope of the life to come— one in which we enjoy Eden restored. Although, for now, we are tested as gold refined by fire, we know even the pain can be used for our good.

We can always rejoice in God's goodness and steadfast love toward us. Joy is a fruit of the Spirit and thus is not dependent upon certain conditions. It is rooted in the imperishable, unchanging, and unconditional. As long as we have the Spirit, we can have eyes to see the Lord's goodness in the land of the living. And in seeing, we can rejoice.

Peter goes on to say (in 1 Pet. 1:10-12) that as children of God after Christ's coming and ascension, we have the benefit of knowing who Christ is, how He suffered, and how He was resurrected three days later. These are things the prophets foretold but never saw with their own eyes and things "into which angels long to look" (1 Pet. 1:12). We may not have seen these things with our eyes but we have the witness of Scripture and the thousands upon thousands of faithful saints who have gone before us.

What does Hebrews 11:1 say faith is?

Hebrews 11 continues with the "hall of faith"—a recounting of the faithful who believed in the coming of Christ without seeing it with their own eyes. I like how *The Message* translates verses 13-16:

Each one of these people of faith died not yet having in hand what was promised, but still believing. How did they do it? They saw it way off in the distance, waved their greeting, and accepted the fact that they were transients in this world. People who live this way make it plain that they are looking for their true home. If they were homesick for the old country, they could have gone back any time they wanted. But they were after a far better country than that—heaven country. You can see why God is so proud of them, and has a City waiting for them.

Rejoicing and faith go hand in hand. If we are to rejoice always, it is imperative to believe that there is more than what we can see, taste, smell, hear, and feel. There simply has to be more. Praise God, there is.

I don't know which season of distress you may be in, if one at all, but if you are, how can you fulfill God's will for your life to "rejoice always"?

It may feel cruel of God to insist that you "rejoice always," especially if you are enduring an incredibly painful trial. Because we know God is for us (Rom. 8:31), we can know that His will for us to rejoice always is for our good. Remember, this isn't a "don't worry, be happy" rejoicing. This is a "though you are grieved you can take delight in what is to come" kind of rejoicing.

How do you think rejoicing despite our circumstances is for our good?

Take this time, as we close, to delight in what the Lord is doing in spite of and through the trials.

Day Three
PRAYER AND THANKS

*Look back at yesterday's homework and write the second exhortation
listed in 1 Thessalonians 5:16-17 here.*

If you are like me, prayer can be hard and somewhat ambiguous. I rarely feel like
I pray enough and even when I do, I wonder if I'm doing it right. So, how on earth
are we to pray without ceasing? The phrase "without ceasing" in the Greek is a
hyperbole.[3] What is meant here is that prayer shouldn't be limited to prescribed
times in the gathering at church or around a table before a meal, but should be
integrated into all of life.

Is prayer easy or difficult for you? Why or why not?

Before we get into the pragmatics of prayer, let's focus on why we pray.

PRAYER IS FELLOWSHIP WITH GOD.

How strong would my marriage be if I never actually talked to Matt or listened
to what he had to say? Could we even have a relationship? What if all I did was
listen to what everyone else had to say about who Matt is but never really got to
know him myself? I could know a lot about him but I wouldn't actually know him.
The same is true about the Lord. Yes, we know Him through His Word but we
interact with Him by talking to and listening to Him through prayer.

*Is it true of you that you know more about God than you know Him? If not,
how have you grown in that?*

PRAYER IS A BECKONING TO JOIN WITH GOD IN ACCOMPLISHING HIS ETERNAL PURPOSES.

What does Jesus say to pray for in Matthew 6:10?

Few things are as sure as praying for God's kingdom to come and His will to be done. Maybe you're asking yourself, *then why pray?* The Lord invites us to join with Him in praying a prayer He is delighted to answer. When we pray for His kingdom to come and His will to be done, it starts to shape our desires and sharpen our vision. We feel a part of what He is doing on earth. When we pray for our neighbors to come to know Him, we begin to take special care of our interaction with them. An affection can start to grow toward those for whom we are praying. We don't just see them as people who happen to live near us, but rather souls whom the Lord divinely placed us close to in order for them to know the steadfast love of Christ for them.

How has praying "God's kingdom come and will be done" shaped your desire and sharpened your vision?

GOD WORKS THROUGH PRAYER.

What does James 5:16-18 say about prayer?

Have you personally seen God change something or someone in answer to your prayers?

Prayer is a means of confession and fighting sin. We just looked at James 5 where we are told to confess our sins to one another and pray for one another so that we may be healed. Again, in Matthew 6, Jesus shows us how prayer is a means of fighting temptation.

Write Matthew 6:13.

Has this been true for you? How so?

Prayer is an act of humility. Too often I neglect prayer because, ever so subtly, I am convinced that I have enough control in a situation to affect a desirable outcome. In other words I'm saying, "It's alright, God. I got this one." Here's how it can look for me:

"It's alright, God. I can try to be a good wife and do all the good wifely things so that my husband, and therefore You, are pleased."

"It's alright, God. I can just try to have more patience with my children. Maybe I won't ruin them forever. Maybe if I read the right Bible stories, pray the right bedtime prayers and be a good, happy Mommy, they'll know You."

"It's alright, God. I can give good enough advice and the perfect Bible verse to a struggling saint so that she can struggle well."

Now, I'm not saying that any of the above actions are bad. On the contrary, they are all good and wise things. However, it's where I am starting that is sinful. I'm not beginning with Him, His Son's work on the cross, and the Spirit's power. I'm beginning with me—what I can do. To put it simply, I am prideful and presumptuous.

It's your turn. List three "I've got this" statements you find yourself either speaking with your mouth or your actions.

1.

2.

3.

Now, turn those into "I need you, Lord" prayers:

1.

2.

3.

Prayer sharpens our sight. It puts prescriptive lenses on our spiritual eyes. An open line of communication with the Lord allows us to "cry out" in our distress and shortsightedness and to hear and see His response. When I am consciously aware of God's presence and am in conversation with Him all throughout the day, inconveniences become opportunities, disappointments become an occasion to trust the Lord's sovereignty, hurts become a chance to extend the forgiveness extended to me through Christ, fears are overcome by His love for me as His child, and happiness overflows into praise. It's not easy, and it's for sure not natural, but it is essential to the next part of His will for my life: to give thanks in all circumstances.

THANKS

Gratitude is a response to God's grace. Karl Barth explains:

> Grace and gratitude belong together like heaven and earth. Grace evokes gratitude like the voice of an echo. Gratitude follows grace like thunder lightning. ... We are speaking of the grace of God who is God for man, and of the gratitude of man as his response to this grace. ... The two belong together, so that only gratitude can correspond to grace, and this correspondence cannot fail.[4]

When we rejoice always and pray without ceasing, we have eyes with lenses adjusted to count God's grace and respond with its echo—gratitude. Our sight is set on the "God who is God *for* man," not against man. All circumstances are occasions to identify God's grace toward us and to thank Him for it.

Go back to Psalm 107:33-35 and complete the following:

He turns _____ into a _____,
_____ of _____ into _____ ground,
a _____ land into a _____ _____,
because of the _____ of its _____.
He turns a _____ into _____ of _____,
a _____ land into _____ of _____.

How might you put that passage in your own words with your prayer spectacles perched atop your nose, able to see God's grace even here?

The Lord of steadfast love knows exactly what we need when we need it. He will dry up our broken wells, expose our chains, lay our earthly wisdom to waste, and pluck up our false anchors. He will also replace our broken wells with the true fountain of His grace. He will break the chains of our rebellion and hurt. He will cover our inadequate knowledge with His unfathomable wisdom. He will be the sure, stable, and steadfast anchor in the storm.

We can give thanks for the hard things because we can see His grace even there. And when He delivers us from the season of distress, our thanks is amplified because we've seen the depths in the desert, chains, folly, and storm, and He came through for us. Gratitude grows when we know how much we don't deserve it. One of my favorite stories in the Bible highlights this truth.

PRODIGAL GOD

Read Luke 15:11-32.

I've borrowed a phrase from Dr. Timothy Keller to describe the Lord in this passage, *Prodigal God.*[5] Often we hear this story called The Prodigal Son. For one last time, open up a dictionary, and write down the definition of *prodigal*.

Prodigal:

In light of what you found, why could this be an adjective for the son? Why might it be an adjective for God?

What happens to the prodigal son? What does it say he did in verse 17?

How did the prodigal son think his father would react? How did his father actually react?

God may send a famine; He may dry up our rivers. But He's also the loving Father who runs toward His sons and daughters even while they are a long way off.

- -

When they are diminished and brought low
through oppression, evil, and sorrow,
he pours contempt on princes
and makes them wander in trackless wastes;
but he raises up the needy out of affliction
and makes their families like flocks.
The upright see it and are glad,
and all wickedness shuts its mouth.

PSALM 107:39-42

- -

There's another son in this story. Who is he and how does he react to the father's prodigal love for the younger son? Why do you think he reacted this way?

With whom do you sympathize most? Why?

Here's the truth: In order for the younger son to be welcomed back into the family, the older son had to give up part of the inheritance left to him. The coat, the ring, the food, and the fattened calf would all be his when his father died. Now, they have been lavished on his foolish little brother. Sound familiar? In this story, the older brother acts badly. But in the True Story, Jesus is the older brother who gives up His life so that we—the foolish little brothers and sisters—can share in the inheritance. We are accepted, clothed, and celebrated at His expense. He paid the price for the grace we freely receive. His righteousness covers our unrighteousness. His blood atones for our sin. We walk in the newness of life because we no longer live, but Christ lives in us. And the life we now live in the flesh we live by faith in the Son of God, who loved us and gave Himself for us. His affliction became our admission. All wickedness shuts its mouth because it has no case to bring against us. Christ paid for it.

Pen a prayer of thanksgiving to the Lord for such grace.

Day Four
SAY SO

- -

Oh give thanks to the LORD, for he is good,
for his steadfast love endures forever!
Let the redeemed of the LORD say so,
whom he has redeemed from trouble
and gathered in from the lands,
from the east and from the west,
from the north and from the south.

PSALM 107:1-3

- -

We are back where we started—back to square one (or, rather, verse 1), but hopefully with a keener sense of the Lord's steadfast love for us. Remember our old nemesis from Week One, Day Five? Read what Revelation 12:10-11 has to say about him:

- -

And I heard a loud voice in heaven, saying, "Now the salvation and
the power and the kingdom of our God and the authority of his
Christ have come, for the accuser of our brothers has been thrown
down, who accuses them day and night before our God. And they
have conquered him by the blood of the Lamb and by the word of
their testimony, for they loved not their lives even unto death."

- -

How does it say they conquered the one "who accuses them day and night before our God"?

Does the description of the accuser sound familiar (from Job)?

In Job 1, Satan (the accuser) is seen presenting himself before the Lord with "the sons of God." God draws attention to Job and Satan accuses Job of being so hedged by God's protection that he would surely cease to fear God if it were removed. A season of much distress and loss commences for Job, but only what the Lord would allow. At the end, it says Job's fortunes are restored and the Lord gives him twice as much as he had before.

How do you think we even know of Job's story?

Someone had to tell it, didn't they? My guess, with the intimacy of the conversation between the Lord and Job, is that Job told it to someone. By the inspiration of the Holy Spirit, whoever recorded it did so for the glory of God and to tell Job's story.

You, like Job, have a story too. You, the redeemed from trouble, have the opportunity and the joy to tell it.

Write 2 Corinthians 1:3-4 below:

I want to give you the time and space today to tell your story. What has the Lord done in you these past weeks we've had together? What comfort have you received in your affliction that you can use to "say so"? How has the Lord shown you His steadfast love? Go back over your homework and draw out a few things. Then, in the following space, write your story of redemption.

I pray this exercise strengthened your faith and caused worship and gratitude to pour out of you! We're almost done but there's still more. Tomorrow is looking bittersweet!

- -

Whoever is wise, let him attend to these things;
let them consider the steadfast love of the LORD.

PSALM 107:43

- -

Day Five
WHAT'S NEXT?

Not only do we have our own stories to tell, we have our own ways of telling them. You have been given gifts, abilities, and opportunities that are only yours. Today, I am going to take you to a story you've probably heard before if you've spent much time in church.

Read Matthew 25:14-30.

In the past, I have erroneously confused "talents" in this parable with natural talents. Here, the term is describing the highest denomination of money in that time. This term also represents a valuable resource, not purely an aptitude. A talent includes, but is not limited to, natural ability, gifts, and opportunities.

What are your thoughts as you read the master's response to each servant?

I always felt bad for the guy with one talent. I mean, he already only has one talent. Can you blame him for being a little hesitant to risk losing it?

Eugene Peterson comes through again with his translation and interpretation of the text in *The Message*:

"The servant given one thousand said, 'Master, I know you have high standards and hate careless ways, that you demand the best and make no allowances for error. I was afraid I might disappoint you, so I found a good hiding place and secured your money. Here it is, safe and sound down to the last cent.'

The master was furious. 'That's a terrible way to live! It's criminal to live cautiously like that! If you knew I was after the best, why did you do less than the least? The least you could have done would have been to invest the sum with the bankers, where at least I would have gotten a little interest.

'Take the thousand and give it to the one who risked the most. And get rid of this "play-it-safe" who won't go out on a limb. Throw him out into utter darkness.'"

MATTHEW 25:24-30 (emphasis mine)

This cuts me to the core. Countless times I have thought, it's not worth doing unless I do it perfectly, so I'd better not even try! By thinking and acting upon this, I reveal that I don't trust the Lord's goodness and power. I don't trust that His grace is sufficient even if I fail. I have hoarded my natural abilities, gifts, and opportunities out of fear—fear of failure and disapproval. This proves I don't really know Him. But to risk my talent—whether it's one or five—shows that I know Him and His character. Investing my talent and going out on a limb with what He has entrusted to me is an opportunity to enter His joy and partner with Him in what's next.

Has fear kept you from investing your abilities, gifts, and opportunities? Fear of what?

All right, it's your turn (again). You have a story. You have "talents." Take some time to consider how you will invest them. No dream is too big or too small. What is He putting on your heart to do/be a part of?

Now:

One year from now:

Five years from now:

Ten years from now:

We can't see into the future. We don't even know what tomorrow may hold, but what we do know is that God is the Lord of steadfast love who is for us. This means we can dream without guilt and without clenching our hands tightly. We dream freely because we are so freely loved.

Not all of our deserts, chains, folly, and storms are behind us. They will come again, but don't be discouraged. Each season is an opportunity to reveal the anchor of our souls. There's no fear for the one who fears the Lord, for the one whose soul is anchored in His steadfast love.

Share with your group or someone you trust what the Lord has shown you today. Have them pray with you and hold you accountable to put steps to it. Let the redeemed of the Lord say so in the way and spaces He has ordained for you!

Week Seven

GOODBYES ARE HARD.

Let the redeemed of the LORD say so,
    whom he has redeemed from trouble
and gathered in from the lands,
    from the east and from the west,
    from the north and from the south.

PSALM 107:2-3

DISCUSSION QUESTIONS:

What spoke to you in Eugene Peterson's quote about how God creates us all uniquely?

What has God initiated in your life over the last several weeks?

No one else has your story—you are original. How is God leading you to be the redeemed who says so?

LEADER GUIDE

Steadfast Love is a video and discussion based Bible study that can be used in a variety of small or large group settings, including churches, homes, offices, or coffee shops. The weekly personal study along with the teaching videos will promote honest conversation as you study Scripture together in a group. Since conversation is essential to the experience, a few starter questions have been provided in both the Viewer Guides and Leader Guide to help get the discussion rolling.

TIPS ON LEADING THIS BIBLE STUDY

PRAY

As you prepare to lead *Steadfast Love*, remember that prayer is essential. Set aside time each week to pray for the women in your group. Listen to their needs and the struggles they're facing so you can bring them before the Lord. Though organizing and planning are important, protect your time of prayer before each gathering. Encourage your women to include prayer as part of their own daily spiritual discipline as well.

GUIDE

Accept women where they are, but also set expectations that motivate commitment. You can borrow the phrase I've used throughout the study—it's okay to not be okay, but it's not okay to stay there. Be consistent and trustworthy as a leader. Encourage women to follow through on the study, attend the group sessions, and engage with the homework. Listen carefully, responsibly guide discussion, and keep confidences shared within the group. Be honest and vulnerable by sharing what God is teaching you through the study. Most women will follow your lead and be more willing to share and participate when they see your transparency. Reach out to women of different ages, backgrounds, and stages of life. This is sure to make your conversation and experience richer.

CONNECT

Stay engaged with the women in your group. Use social media, texts, emails, or a quick note in the mail to connect with them and share prayer needs throughout the week. Let them know when you're praying specifically for them. Root everything in Scripture and encourage them in their relationships with Jesus.

CELEBRATE

At the end of the study, celebrate what God has done by having your group share what they've learned and how they've grown. Pray together about further steps God may be asking you each to take as a result of this study.

TIPS ON ORGANIZING THIS BIBLE STUDY

- Talk to your pastor or minister of education. Ask for their input, prayers, and support, especially if you're leading this group as a part of your local church.

- Secure your location. Think about the number of women you can accomodate in the designated location. Reserve any tables, chairs, or media equipment for the videos, music, and any additional audio needs.

- Provide childcare. If you are targeting moms of young children and/or single moms, this is essential.

- Provide resources. Order leader kits and the needed number of Bible study books. You might get a few extra for the last minute sign-ups.

- Plan and prepare. Become familiar with the Bible study and leader helps available. Preview the video session and prepare the outline you will follow to lead each group meeting. Go to *lifeway.com/steadfastlove* to find free extra leader and promotional resources for your study.

EVALUATE

At the end of each group session ask: What went well? What could be improved? Did you see women's lives transformed? Did your group grow closer to Christ and to one another?

NEXT STEPS

After the study concludes, follow up and challenge women to stay involved through another Bible study, church opportunity, or anything that will continue friendships and their spiritual growth. Provide several options of ministry opportunities members can participate in individually or as a group to apply what they have learned through this study.

SESSION 1

1. Welcome women to the study and distribute Bible study books.

2. Watch the Session 1 video, encouraging women to take notes as Lauren teaches.

3. Following the video, lead women through the Discussion Questions on the Week 1 Viewer Guide (page 12).

4. Close the session with prayer.

SESSION 2

1. Welcome women to Session 2 of *Steadfast Love*.

2. Ask for a volunteer to Psalm 107 aloud.

3. Use the following questions to review the previous week's personal study.

What are some of the nicknames you've had? How do they accurately (or inaccurately) describe you?

Which name of God struck you this week? How does knowing some of His names affect your relationship with Him?

On Day Two, we talked about what we worship. If you feel comfortable sharing with the group, talk about what you learned from the questions to determine your object of worship.

What did you learn about covenants this week that you didn't already know? What does that teach you about who God is?

4. Watch the Session 2 video, encouraging women to take notes as Lauren teaches.

5. Following the video, lead women through the Discussion Questions on the Week 2 Viewer Guide (page 36).

6. Pray, thanking Jesus for meeting you at your well. Thank Him for inviting you, thirsty, to come to Him.

SESSION 3

1. Welcome women to Session 3 of *Steadfast Love*.

2. Split into smaller groups (between two and three people) and have the groups read Psalm 107 aloud to one another.

3. Use the following questions to review the previous week's personal study.

   Which mark of the desert—lonely, longing, lament—do you find yourself seeing most often in your life? Why do you think that is?

   How would you describe the purpose of an anchor? Of a well?

   Are you in a desert right now? How can our group be praying for you this week?

   How have you seen people be the hands and feet of God for you?

4. Watch the Session 3 video, encouraging women to take notes as Lauren teaches.

5. Following the video, lead women through the Discussion Questions on the Week 3 Viewer Guide (page 68).

6. Lead a time of prayer, inviting women to surrender their chains to Christ. Praise Him for delighting in breaking our chains, for His grace that is sufficient for us!

NOTE: *If you are experiencing physical or emotional abuse, please get safe and get help. The following hotlines will provide help for you: Domestic Violence 24-Hour Hotline (800-799-7233), Runaways Hotline (888-580-4357), Social Security Hotline (800-772-1213).*

The following resources help those who may be struggling with substance abuse: Recovering Redemption and Steps by Matt Chandler, Women Reaching Women in Crisis by Chris Adams, Breaking Free and Living Free by Beth Moore, Celebrate Recovery Programs.

SESSION 4

1. Welcome women to Session 4 of *Steadfast Love.*

2. Divide Psalm 107 into smaller sections and ask for a few volunteers to read each section aloud.

3. Use the following questions to review the previous week's personal study.

   Have you ever accepted Jesus' rescue? If so, share your story with the group.

   What did you read and learn from Scripture this week that encouraged you about your hurts, hooks, and hang ups?

   What does it mean to you to know that we worship the Most High God?

4. Watch the Session 4 video, encouraging women to take notes as Lauren teaches.

5. Following the video, lead women through the Discussion Questions on the Week 4 Viewer Guide (page 98).

6. Provide an opportunity for women to pair up and confess to one another, praying together to close the session.

SESSION 5

1. Welcome women to Session 5 of *Steadfast Love.*

2. Ask for a volunteer to read Psalm 107 aloud.

3. Use the following questions to review the previous week's personal study.

   What is folly?

   What does it mean to fear the Lord? How does that combat folly in our lives?

   Which of God's attributes speaks to you the most where you are right now? Why?

How do you dive into God's Word to know Him more? Do you have a plan that works for you? Share it with the group and help one another stay accountable to be in God's Word.

4. Watch the Session 5 video, encouraging women to take notes as Lauren teaches.

5. Following the video, lead women through the Discussion Questions on the Week 5 Viewer Guide (page 130). This week's discussion questions are difficult. Be sensitve to those in the midst of storms who may not yet have the hope of Christ.

6. Invite women to accept the hope of the gospel. Pray for those in the midst of storms, that they may know God's presence. Praise God for His presence and His grace in the midst of a storm.

SESSION 6

1. Welcome women to Session 6 of *Steadfast Love*.

2. Split into groups and ask the women to read Psalm 107 aloud to one another—or recite parts from memory! This is a no-pressure activity, but since we've read it several times each week, you may know some stanzas by heart.

3. Use the following questions to review the previous week's personal study.

How does what we fear reveal our faith?

What did you learn new this week about Jonah?

How is Jesus the better Jonah?

Tim Keller says, "God will only give you what you would have asked for if you knew everything He knows." Does this bring you comfort? Why or why not?

4. Watch the Session 6 video, encouraging women to take notes as Lauren teaches.

5. Following the video, lead women through the Discussion Questions on the Week 6 Viewer Guide (page 158).

6. Practice gratitude by giving thanks to God for loving us enough to prove that He is enough, that He loves with a steadfast love. Challenge the women to write out their prayers of thanksgiving somewhere, either in their Bible study books or in a separate journal.

SESSION 7

1. Welcome women to Session 7 of *Steadfast Love.*

2. Read Psalm 107 aloud.

3. Use the following questions to review the previous week's personal study.

Name something that reminds you of a time when God delievered you from a desert, chains, folly, or a storm.

In your current season, how can you fulfill God's will for your life to "rejoice always"?

Have you seen a prayer answered in your life or in the life of someone you know? Share with the group.

What is one thing God showed you or did for you through this study that you plan to "say so" about?

If you're willing, share your ideas as to how you might invest the talents and story with which God has entrusted you (page 180) and ask the group to help hold you accountable to your action steps.

4. Watch the Session 7 video, encouraging women to take notes as Lauren teaches.

5. Following the video, lead women through the Discussion Questions on the Week 7 Viewer Guide (page 184).

6. Following the discussion, spend some time allowing women to share what they gained from this study. Ask: which week spoke to them the most? Which verses in Psalm 107 ministered to them during this season? Have they memorized any of the verses? Pray together thanking God for His steadfast love and asking Him to help you live out what you've learned.

7. Brainstorm together ways to continue the ministry started in the group. Extend an invitation to a mission project or another Bible study. Say "see you later"!

ENDNOTES

INTRODUCTION

1. "Definition of Invoke," accessed March 16, 2017, *dictionary.com/browse/invoke* © 2016 Dictionary. com, LLC.

WEEK ONE

1. Lecrae Moore, Twitter post, March 31, 2013, 8:28 a.m., twitter. com/lecrae.

2. "Definition of Worship," accessed March 20, 2017, *dictionary.com/browse/worship?s=t* © 2016 Dictionary. com, LLC.

3. *Quote adapted from a statement by Bruce Leafblad.* Rick Melson, "Worship: Our Response to His Greatness," *Desiring God blog*, April 3, 2016, accessed March 20, 2017. Available online at *desiringgod. org/articles/worship-our-response-to-his-greatness*

4. Jennifer Dukes Lee, *Love Idol: Letting Go of Your Need for Approval and Seeing Yourself through God's Eyes* (Carol Stream, Illinois: Tyndale, 2014), 47.

5. James Strong, *Strong's Exhaustive Concordance of the Bible*, accessed on March 20, 2017, via *blueletterbible. org/lang/lexicon/lexicon. cfm?Strongs=H3290&t=KJV*

6. James Strong, *Strong's Exhaustive Concordance of the Bible*, accessed on March 20, 2017, via *blueletterbible. org/lang/Lexicon/Lexicon. cfm?strongs=H8095&t=KJV*

7. David Brown, *A is for Adam, E is for Eve: A Biblical Guide for Naming Your Child*; (Mustang, Oklahoma: Tate Publishing & Enterprises, LLC, 2009), 61.

8. James Strong, *Strong's Exhaustive Concordance of the Bible*, accessed on March 20, 2017, via *blueletterbible. org/lang/lexicon/lexicon. cfm?Strongs=G3972&t=KJV*

9. Alexander MacLaren, *MacLaren's Expositions Of Holy Scripture*, accessed on March 20, 2017, via *biblehub.com/commentaries/acts/13-9.htm*

10. "The Names of God in the Old Testament," accessed

on March 20, 2017, via *blueletterbible.org/study/misc/ name_god.cfm* ©2017 Blue Letter Bible

11. Ibid.

12. John Piper, "10 Things 'Yahweh' Means," *Desiring God blog*, August 5, 2016, accessed on March 20, 2017. Available online at *desiringgod.org/ articles/10-things-yahweh-means*

13. Chad Brand, Charles Draper, Archie England, ed., *Holman Illustrated Bible Dictionary* (Nashville: Holman Bible Publishers, 2003), accessed via *mywsb.com*.

14. Ibid.

15. R. J. Thompson, *Penitence and Sacrifice in Early Israel Outside the Levitical Law: An Examination of the Fellowship Theory of Early Israelite Sacrifice* (Netherlands: E.J. Brill: 1963), 55.

16. Ibid, Brand, Draper, and England.

17. Ibid, Brand, Draper, and England.

18. John Piper, "Job: Reverent in Suffering," *Desiring God*, July 7, 1985, accessed on March 27, 2017. Available online at

desiringgod.org/messages/ job-reverent-in-suffering

19. Aaron Keyes, Jack Mooring, Bryan Brown, *Sovereign Over Us*. Brentwood, TN: Thankyou Music, 2011.

WEEK TWO

1. Charles Spurgeon, *The Treasury of David* (Grand Rapids: Kregel Publications, 1968) accessed via *mywsb.com*.

2. "Living With Wolves: Vocalization," accessed on March 21, 2017, via *livingwithwolves. org/about-wolves/language/* © 2017 Living with Wolves.

3. John D. Barry, ed., *The Lexham Bible Dictionary* (Bellingham, WA: Lexham Press, 2016), accessed via *Logos*.

4. Ibid.

5. Chad Brand, Charles Draper, Archie England, ed., *Holman Illustrated Bible Dictionary* (Nashville: Holman Bible Publishers, 2003), accessed via *mywsb.com*.

6. George Wigram, *The Englishman's Greek Concordance of New Testament* accessed March 27, 2017, via Bible Hub. Available online

at *http://biblehub.com/hebrew/ strongs_3477.htm*

7. Brown, Driver, Briggs and Gesenius, *The NAS Old Testament Hebrew Lexicon* accessed on March 27, 2017 via Bible Study Tools. Available online at *biblestudytools.com/ lexicons/hebrew/nas/yashar.html* © 2017, Bible Study Tools.

WEEK THREE

1. Herbert Lockyer, *All the Divine Names and Titles in the Bible* (Grand Rapids: Zondervan, 1975), 9.

2. Wayne Grudem, *Christian Beliefs* (Grand Rapids: Zondervan, 2005), 27.

3. Eugene H. Peterson, *Christ Plays in Ten Thousand Places: A Conversation in Spiritual Theology* (Grand Rapids: Wm. B. Eerdmans Publishing Co., 2005), 7.

4. "Interlinear Breakdown of Colossians 1:13" accessed on March 27, 2017, via Blue Letter Bible. Available online at *blueletterbible.org/kjv/ col/1/12/t_conc_1108013*

5. Robert W. Wall, *The IVP New Testament Commentary Series Colossians and Philemon* (Downers Grove, IL: InterVarsity Press, 1993) via *mywsb.com.*

WEEK FOUR

1. "Definition of folly," *Dictionary. com* Available online at *dictionary.com/browse/folly?s=t;* Merriam-Webster's Dictionary Available online at *merriam- webster.com/dictionary/folly,* accessed on March 27, 2017.

2. Greg Groogan, "Suffering on the San Jacinto: 11 voices" *Fox 26* January 11, 2017, accessed on April 6, 2017. Available online at *fox26houston.com/news/ local-news/228378592-story.*

3. James Strong, *Strong's Exhaustive Concordance of the Bible*, accessed on March 20, 2017, via *Blue Letter Bible* Available online at *blueletterbible. org/lang/lexicon/lexicon. cfm?Strongs=H6031&t=HCSB*

4. Michael Pollan, *In Defense of Food: An Eater's Manifesto* (New York: The Penguin Group, 2008).

5. John Piper, "A Woman Who Fears the Lord Is to Be Praised: Mother's Day," *Desiring God*, May 10, 1981, accessed on March 27, 2017. Available online at *desiringgod.org/messages/a- woman-who-fears-the-lord-is- to-be-praised*

6. "Practical Implications of the Incommunicable Attributes of God" and "Practical Implications of the Communicable Attributes of God" *ESV Study Bible* (Wheaton, Illinois: Crossway Bibles, 2008), 2511-2512 via *mywsb.com.*

7. Matthew Henry, *Matthew Henry's Commentary on the Whole Bible*; (Peabody, MA: Hendrickson Publishers, 1994), 1089 via *mywsb.com.*

8. Joseph Exell and Henry Donald Maurice Spence-Jones, eds., *Pulpit Commentary*, accessed on March 27, 2017, via *http://biblehub.com/commentaries/pulpit/psalms/107.htm.*

WEEK FIVE

1. Gordon Matthew Thomas Sumner "Sting," *Fragile*. Santa Monica, CA: A&M Records, 1988.

2. C.S. Lewis, *The Problem of Pain* (New York: HarperCollins, 1940), 92.

3. J.I. Packer, *Knowing God Through the Year* (Downers Grove, IL: InterVarsity Press, 2004), 81.

4. "Definition of Narcissism" *Dictionary.com* accessed on March 31, 2017. Available online at *dictionary.com/browse/narcissism.*

5. Timothy Keller, Twitter post, April 25, 2013, 8:30 a.m., twitter.com/timkellernyc.

WEEK SIX

1. Hayyim Schauss, *The Jewish Festivals: A Guide to Their History and Observance* (New York: Schocken Books, 1938), 39, 40-41, 87, 89, 117, 118, 125, 171, 200, 237, 250.

2. Charles A. Wanamaker, *The New International Greek Testament Commentary: The Epistles to the Thessalonians, A Commentary on the Greek Text* (Grand Rapids: Wm. B. Eerdmans Publishing Co., 1990), 200. Accessed via *mywsb.com.*

3. William Swam Plumer, *Commentary on Paul's Epistle to the Romans With an Introduction on the Life, Times, Writings and Character of Paul* (New York: Anson D. F. Randolph & Co., 1871), 47.

4. Karl Barth, *Church Dogmatics: The Doctrine of Reconciliation, Volume 4, Part 1: The Doctrine of Reconciliation* (London: T&T Clark International, 1956), 41.

5. Timothy Keller, *The Prodigal God: Recovering the Heart of the Christian Faith* (New York: Riverhead Books, 2008).

NOTES

NOTES

We'll put the kettle on.

The kind of conversation you'd have over tea with your best friend. That's the LifeWay Women blog.

Drop by to grow in your faith, develop as a leader, and find encouragement as you go.

Find Bible studies, events, giveaways, and more at **LifeWayWomen.com**

Sign up for our weekly newsletter at LifeWay.com/WomensNews

LifeWay. | **Women**

Memorize
Psalm 107!

Join the 2-week Scripture Memory Challenge to commit Psalm 107 to memory.

LifeWayWomen.com/Psalm107

#Psalm107Challenge

Sign up to receive a simple plan, memorization tips, and daily encouragement!

LifeWay | Women

"Sometimes He wrings the worship

From our hearts"

There are times when worship overflows easily and effortlessly from a heart full of gratitude and praise. Yet, there are other times when God seems far and we feel we have nothing left to offer. We are tired, or thirsty, or imprisoned in our own chains through our own devices, or caught in the waves of a tumultuous sea. This is when God shows us His steadfast love.

He wraps His eternally powerful, ultimately creative, nail-scarred hands around our hearts and squeezes with appropriate might— yielding an honest plea for Him to save us and deliver us from our circumstances, fears, and self control. And He does. He initiates with His steadfast love, and responds with the same.

Walk with Lauren as she shares what she has learned of the steadfast love of the Lord.

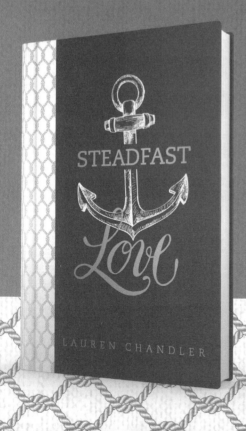

ISBN 978-1433683787
SteadfastLoveBook.com

B&H
Every WORD Matters™
BHPublishingGroup.com